UNFINISHED
EVANGELISM

Y0-BRF-967

UNFINISHED EVANGELISM

TIM WRIGHT

MINNEAPOLIS

UNFINISHED EVANGELISM
More Than Getting Them in the Door

Copyright © 1995 Augsburg Fortress. All rights reserved. Except for brief quotations in critical articles and reviews, no part of this book may be reproduced in any manner without prior written permission from the publisher. Write to: Permissions, Augsburg Fortress, 426 S. Fifth St., Box 1209, Minneapolis, MN 55440.

Scripture quotations unless otherwise noted are from the New Revised Standard Version Bible, copyright © 1989 Division of Christian Education of the National Council of the Churches of Christ in the United States of America. Used by permission. Scripture quotations marked NIV are from The Holy Bible, New International Version, copyright © 1973, 1978, 1984 International Bible Society. Used by permission of Zondervan Bible Publishers.

Cover design: Cindy Cobb-Olson
Text design: James F. Brisson

Library of Congress Cataloging-in-Publication Data

Wright, Tim, 1957–
    Unfinished evangelism : more than getting them in the door / by
Tim Wright.
        p.   cm.
    Includes bibliographical references.
    ISBN 0-8066-2794-8 (alk. paper)
    1. Church work with new church members—United States.
    2. Converts—United States—Religious life.   3. United States—
Religion—1960-   I. Title.
    BV4520.W75   1995
    269'.2—dc20   94-43567
                                                              CIP

The paper used in this publication meets the minimum requirements of American National Standard for Information Sciences—Permanence of Paper for Printed Library Materials, ANSI Z329.48-1984.   ∞™

Manufactured in the U.S.A.   AF 10-27948

99   98   97   96   95   1   2   3   4   5   6   7   8   9   10

•

To Jan, Alycia, and Mike:

I LOVE YOU

•

CONTENTS

•

ACKNOWLEDGMENTS

•

THANKS:

To my family for their love, support, and encouragement.

To the staff and family of Community Church of Joy for their input into the ideas offered in this book.

To Beth Gaede and the staff at Augsburg Fortress, Publishers for their belief in me.

To George Hunter, Lyle Schaller, Kent Hunter, and Bill Easum for their friendship, encouragement, and listening ears over the course of my ministry.

To those who reviewed the manuscript and offered helpful suggestions on how to improve the book.

To all of the mission-driven congregations whose stories are told in this book, for their willingness to change for the sake of the Gospel.

To my Meyers Parrot, Briggs, who faithfully sat on my shoulder keeping me company during the long hours of typing on my PC.

To Jesus Christ, the Author and Perfecter of our faith.

●

O God, from my youth you have
taught me,
and I still proclaim your wondrous deeds.
So even to old age and gray hairs,
O God, do not forsake me,
until I proclaim your might
to all the generations to come.

—PSALM 71:17-18

●

AN INVITATION

•

For the Son of Man came to seek out and to save the lost.

(LUKE 19:10)

Sarah came home from her Lutheran preschool asking questions of faith her mom, Ginny, couldn't answer. Ginny's own faith journey, up to that point, had been pretty limited. As a little girl she attended a Baptist Sunday school with some friends. In seventh grade she spent time hanging out at dances sponsored by the Congregational church. When she turned 16 she decided to join a Methodist youth group. Since the Methodist church was the church farthest from her home in town, going there gave her a great excuse for borrowing the car. When she and her husband-to-be decided to get married, she went back to the Methodists for the wedding. Yet, for all of her brief encounters with churches over the years, Ginny never attended a Sunday morning worship service. For the most part church played a minor role in her life.

After Ginny became a parent she committed herself to finding the best education possible for her children. She investigated pre-schools much like most people investigate colleges. An educator herself, she had heard good reports about Lutheran schools. So after a thorough search, she enrolled her daughter Sarah in a Lutheran preschool.

13

During the time Sarah attended that preschool, no one ever invited Ginny and her family to church. Ginny had numerous friends who belonged to various congregations. But none of them bothered to ask her to come to worship.

When Sarah started asking faith questions, however, Ginny decided to look for a church. Since Sarah attended a Lutheran school, Ginny thought it best to stick with that denomination. She took out the yellow pages and made a list of the Lutheran churches near her house. Her first and last stop was Community Church of Joy in Glendale, a suburb of Phoenix. Through the warm, relevant, contemporary worship Ginny immediately felt comfortable and at home. Soon her entire family was involved in the church.

During a new member class Ginny signed up to teach Sunday school. Because of her teaching background she felt confident that she could handle the position. As a new volunteer she was encouraged to participate in a citywide teacher-training event. During the training session the speaker gathered the attendees into small groups. Ginny happened to sit next to one of the major leaders of the Sunday school association. The speaker instructed the attendees to turn in their Bibles to 3 John. Ginny opened her Bible—the one the Baptists had given her when she was in second grade. But being new to the faith, she had no idea where to find 3 John. She vaguely remembered Matthew, Mark, Luke, and John, but "this third John character" completely baffled her.

The leader of the Sunday School association noticed Ginny flipping helplessly through the pages of her Bible. So she reached over to Ginny's Bible, found 3 John for her, and pointed to the verse. Ginny was deeply embarrassed and could hardly wait to get out of the meeting. She went back to Joy and promptly resigned her Sunday school position. Many adults, having been similarly embarrassed, would have given up. But the experience had the opposite effect on Ginny. It motivated her to learn as much as she could about the Bible and her new faith.

Eventually Ginny became a member of the church council. That led to her current position as Adult Education Director at her church. As a part of her job she now helps other seekers—like she used to be—become disciples of Jesus Christ.

A NEW AUDIENCE

Ginny represents a growing segment in our society today—a segment mainline churches don't often encounter: unchurched seekers with little or no experience in a Christian community and little or no knowledge of the Christian faith. However, with the decline of mainline denominations and the growing unchurched population, many churches are taking a new look at how to reach people like her.[1] Throughout the country and around the world, congregations are discovering innovative ways to reach the unchurched and helping them grow in the faith.

This book is about building churches for unchurched people. It's written for anyone passionate about seeing people like Ginny transformed by the Gospel. It serves as an invitation to mainline congregations to consider how they might more effectively reach the unchurched—a different audience than many congregations usually serve.

In the following seven chapters the book will:

- present the six building blocks for designing a congregation committed to leading the unchurched into discipleship;
- share insights into how churches can attract unchurched people to its ministry;
- offer practical suggestions for "growing" these newcomers along with the current members; and
- look at the process for bringing about change in a church.

Many of the ideas presented in these pages will help congregations more effectively nurture those already in the church. The primary emphasis of this book, however, is on transforming the church into a mission—and on helping those already committed to the church reach and nurture the unchurched. Each chapter ends with a Dreamshop, a series of questions designed to help a congregation think through and apply the information presented in the chapter.

PRESUPPOSITIONS

The title of the book, *Unfinished Evangelism: More Than Getting Them in the Door*, presupposes the following:

1) That bringing new people into the church without an effective strategy for nurturing them qualifies as unfinished evangelism.

2) That congregations focused only on nurturing "their own" miss the joy of Christ's mandate to go and make disciples.

3) That evangelism is the process of leading the unchurched into a relationship with Christ and the church, building them up in the faith, and sending them out to reach others.

4) That reaching out to the unchurched is the heart of Christ's mission to "seek out and to save the lost."

5) That nurturing believers in a church geared to the unchurched is easier and more effective than trying to reach the unchurched in a congregation focused primarily on its current members.

6) That one of the most effective ways to nurture and energize members is to equip them to invest their lives in reaching out to others.

7) That the congregation is the best place for doing evangelism.

These presuppositions grow, in part, out of my experience as a pastor of an outreach-oriented church. Thirty-eight percent of our members come from a previously unchurched background. Another 22% joined our church after five or more years away from any church involvement. In the chapters that follow I will flesh out these presuppositions, and I will share some of our experiences in building a congregation for unchurched people.

DEFINING TERMS

For purposes of this book the terms "church" and "congregation" mean the same thing. When referring to the universal or worldwide body of believers, I will use "Church" with a capital C.

I will also be interchanging the words "secular," "unchurched," "irreligious," and "seeker." Though they have different nuances, for this book they will essentially describe the same kind of person— one whose life and values are not currently being influenced by the gospel or a local church.

Finally, the underlying bias of this book is that mission—leading seekers into discipleship—is an exciting, revitalizing adventure. This book serves as an invitation to that adventure.

PASSION

•

passion: strong or intense feeling;
strong or ardent liking or enthusiasm;
object of strong feeling;
the sufferings of Jesus Christ.

—MERIT STUDENTS DICTIONARY

CHAPTER 1

IT'S A NEW DAY
AND A NEW WORLD!

•

Those who are well have no need of a
physician, but those who are sick . . . I
have come to call not the righteous but
sinners.

(MATTHEW 9:12-13)

The Church as many of us know it no longer exists! The Church of the 1940s and 1950s, where mainline denominations and congregations enjoyed respect and growth, died in the 1960s. The reason: The world as we know it no longer exists.

Staggering changes have taken place in the world over the last 40 years. These changes, or paradigm shifts, have significant implications for congregations and their ministries.

Over the last 40 years the world has shifted from:

Rural to urban. Before World War II, agriculture played a significant role in the economy and life of the United States. Most people lived in rural communities. They rarely moved to new areas. They developed deep lasting relationships with the community and each other. The success of the farm depended on families sticking together and working together. The rural setting promoted stability and the church served as one anchor of that stability—one expression of that communal mindset.

Today, the overwhelming majority of people live in urban or cosmopolitan areas. City life and the needs growing out of cosmopolitan living differ dramatically from rural life and needs. Urban living often isolates people. Family members are scattered all over the country. Individuality reigns.

Unfortunately, many churches and denominations continue to do ministry with a rural mind-set, even in the city. For example, they design ministries on the assumption of stability. Bible study programs lasting two or more years assume people stay around that long. In reality, people have become increasingly mobile.

Group goals to individual goals. The generation born before World War II thrived on group accomplishments. They believed in team work. They banded together to win world wars, beat the Depression, and build a great nation. They formed the first scouting groups. If sacrifice was called for, it showed itself in the individual sacrificing for the group. While in many ways, rugged individualism defined the United States and its citizens, previous generations still put high value on working together.

The generations born after World War II, Baby Boomers (1946 to 1964) and Baby Busters (1965 to 1976), focus on individual goals. Cheryl Russell, the former editor-inchief of *American Demographics* magazine, calls them the new generations of free agents.[1]

> The term *individualism* is too general to accurately describe how this perspective shapes people's attitudes and behavior. The individuality of Americans under the age of 50 is more accurately described by the term **free agent.** In baseball, basketball, and football, free agents are players who negotiate their contracts as individuals rather than as part of a team. . . . Most Americans under the age of 50 are free agents, negotiating their way through life.[2]

Free agents look out for themselves, often at the expense of the group.

> Modern technology allows individualism to be taken to its extreme. In the information age, people can substitute computers, modems, telephones, faxes, and answering machines for face-to-face contact with others. They can work and play in anonymity. Individualism is the master trend of our time, feeding on the anonymity of the information age.[3]

Free agents do what they want when they want to do it. The symptoms of this mind-set have been devastating: divorce, rising crime rates, addictions, broken homes, latchkey kids, and sexually transmitted diseases, are but a few.

As they age, free agents increasingly find themselves confronted by a difficult challenge: balancing their high sense of individualism with their growing communal responsibilities. Free agents want to pursue their own personal goals and agendas. But those goals and agendas may at times conflict with their responsibility to raise their children, care for aging parents, or contribute to society as volunteers.

The church of the 1950s shaped its ministry around the needs of those born before World War II—a generation of people more committed to a group orientation. For many free agents, a group orientation no longer works. Certainly the gospel calls for self-sacrifice and a communal attitude. However, free agents want to know how the gospel affects them personally before they'll wrestle with its communal implications.

An industrial economy to a personalized economy. Cheryl Russell writes:

> The agricultural economy was based on the production and distribution of food and handcrafted products. The industrial economy was based on the production of mass-produced products. The personalized economy is based on the production of customized products for individualistic consumers. This new economy demands a new way of life.[4]

In a personalized economy people rely on fax machines, cellular phones, television, computer stores, fast food restaurants, and microwave ovens rather than letters, newspapers, family dinners, and conventional ovens.[5] Such an economy values innovation over loyalty, instant action over analysis, and short-term gains over long-term goals.

The customer reigns in the new personalized economy. And just as consumers demand customized products, so they value churches tailored to their needs. Noted Lutheran scholar Martin Marty wisely cautions against catering too much to this consumer mentality by saying,

To give the whole store away to match what this year's market says the unchurched want is to have the people who know the least about faith determine most about its expression.[6]

Congregations eager to make an impact on a secular society take that caution seriously. However, for them the issue is not, "Will we allow those who know the least about faith determine its expression?," but "How do we communicate historic Christianity in such a way that it connects with and transforms a secular culture?"

People serving the institution to the institution serving people. In the 1950s churches grew in part as a result of denominational loyalty. Lutherans joined Lutheran congregations. Presbyterians sought out Presbyterian churches. Loyalty tied people to the institution or denomination. Volunteer recruiting was easier, to a certain degree, because of the loyalty people felt toward the institution. However, trust in institutions is dwindling.

Between 1973 and 1991, the percentage of Americans with a great deal of trust in organized religion fell from 66 to 56 percent. The share who trust the public schools fell from 58 to 35 percent. Trust in the Supreme Court fell from 44 to 39 percent, while trust in Congress fell from 48 to 18 percent. Trust in the presidency hovered at just 50 percent in 1991.[7]

Today, in our highly individualistic society, free agents feel little loyalty to the institution. They care more about how the institution will serve them. During their growing-up years institutions let them down. Many events and issues—from the Viet Nam War and Watergate to increasingly irrelevant churches—have left many free agents feeling alienated. Loyalty to an institution lasts only as long as that institution serves or meets the needs of the customer. Consequently today's free agents are less likely to vote and carry out other civic duties.

Churches can no longer build themselves on denominational loyalty. Today, they have to win people over by responding to their needs in a relevant, life-transforming way.

Standardization to innovation. Generally speaking, a sense of sameness permeated the 1950s and early 1960s. Conformity was in. Men and boys wore similar hairstyles. Clothing styles were more similar than dissimilar. Denominational worship services across the country seemed more alike than different. Standardization was valued.

In the mid-1960s many young Boomer free agents rebelled against such standardization. Males grew out their hair. Young men and women alike rejected the conservative clothes of their parents. Instead they wore "groovy" psychedelic shirts and ragged bell-bottomed jeans. They protested the Viet Nam war. They fought for or against Civil Rights. They rallied around a new kind of music— rock and roll.

Today's free agents value innovation. The new and the up-to-date appeals to them more than the "same old same old." Congregations eager to reach them will find innovative ways to "tell the old, old, story."

Mass market to niche markets. In the 1960s people had basically three television networks from which to choose: CBS, NBC, or ABC. Today, with the advent of cable and satellite, people can choose from 50 or more channels—most of them niched to specific audiences. Broadcasting has been replaced with narrowcasting.

In the 1960s people bought Coke® or Pepsi®. Today they can purchase New Coke®, Diet Coke®, Diet Coke® without caffeine, Classic Coke®, Pepsi®, Diet Pepsi®, Diet Pepsi® without sodium, and so on. The average supermarket now stocks four times as many products as it did in 1950.[8]

One size no longer fits everyone. People today value choices because they've been raised on choices. They want products (or churches) designed around their particular needs. They expect choices in worship styles and programming.

Traditional family life to alternative families. The typical family of the 1950s consisted of a working dad, a housewife mom, and several children. Today the majority of moms work outside the home. Because of divorce and births outside of marriage, blended families and single parent families populate our communities. The number of adults who never marry, and consequently never divorce or experience the death of a spouse, continues to rise. The "traditional family structure" of the 1950s no longer fits the majority of family structures today. Our country and congregations consist of several different family types.

Caring for these new kinds of families means changing the way churches do ministry. For example, we can no longer assume that children will be in Sunday school every week. One week they attend church with mom. The next Sunday they attend dad's church. "Family" activities tend to exclude more people than they include. Treating families with a 1950s mind-set will alienate most people today. Congregations hoping to remain effective into the next century will take these new realities seriously.

Verbal/written communications to visual communications. Some pastors tend to prepare their sermons as if writing for readers, not hearers. The messages sound more like magazine articles, for example, than conversations. Today, people receive communication visually. They see it and hear it rather than read it. People watch CNN and other news networks rather than read the newspaper. A dwindling number of people receive their information from written sources. Today's generations thrive on visual images. To reach them, congregations will want to look for ways to use video, drama, dance, and other visual means to present the message. And the sermon itself should take on a conversational tone rather than a literary one.

Left brain to right brain. The test of truth today is no longer only found in facts (left brain) but in experience (right brain).

Wade Clark Roof, in his excellent book, *A Generation of Seekers: The Spiritual Journeys of the Baby Boom Generation*, writes:

> Individuals are inclined to regard their own experiences as superior to the accounts of others, and the truths found through self-discovery as having greater relevance to them than those handed down by way of creed or custom. Direct experience is always more trustworthy, if for no other reason than because of its "inwardness" and "withiness"—two qualities that have come to be much appreciated in a highly expressive, narcissistic culture.[9]

When trying to reach unchurched people, congregations will do well to find experiential, relevant ways to share the truth of the gospel. For people not only want to know about God, they want to experience God. The issue is not just truth but relevance. Does the gospel make sense? Does it have something to say to my life? Can it make a difference?

Denominations to congregations. At one time denominations inspired loyalty. They held people together across cities and states. They enabled people from all over the country to join together and do something significant. The denominational creed said, "Together we're better."

Today, denominations have lost much of their influence. Cutbacks and tight budgets underscore the problem. Individualists tend to have little appreciation for what the denomination—its staff and headquarters—hundreds of miles from them, is doing. People want to be where the action is. They want to see their money working in their own city.

Denominational headquarters tend to create programs with a one-size-fits-all mentality, understandably so. They have to service hundreds and thousands of congregations. They can't possibly tailor-make programs for each setting. Unfortunately, as stated before, in today's market, many one-size-fits-all programs ultimately fit no one. Denominations committed to growing will look for new, innovative ways to help local congregations create customized programs—programs that grow out of the needs of local communities.

Religion to spirituality. Religious institutions, including churches, offer stability, tradition, history, and systems for meaning. They offer people the chance to join with others to make a difference in the world. However, religion, in the minds of many, has to do with a commitment to a particular institution and the creeds and beliefs of that institution. Such exclusive commitments turn off many individualists.

A growing segment of today's new generations is much more interested in spirituality than in religion. They see spirituality—the inward search for meaning and significance—as a deeply personal experience.

> The world inside the churches and synagogues often seems far removed, if not downright alien, to life as experienced outside; the institutional languages of creed and doctrine often

come across as stale and timeworn . . . Yet as a generation many yearn deeply for a religious experience they can claim as "their own." The yearning for some kind of immediacy is expressed in many ways, in both the traditional and nontraditional languages: centering one's life, focusing within, knowing God, getting in touch with yourself, the higher self, finding "it."[10]

The good news for congregations is that free agents are highly interested in spirituality. Offering aid and support for their spiritual journey will attract some of them to church.

"Christendom" to "secularity."[11] Many people today admit to being on a spiritual journey. That journey, however, is being influenced less and less by Christianity or the Church. Instead, many are turning to "alternative" religions (including eastern religions and the New Age movement). Or they're designing hybrid religions (picking and choosing elements that "feel" right from various world religions). Or they're creating self-generated systems of meaning based on inner fulfillment. In other words, the era of Christendom, in which Christianity shaped Western civilization, is over.

In the Christendom Era, beginning with the conversion of Roman Emperor Constantine in A.D. 313, the Church affected every area of life including philosophy, the arts, and law. During that time the lines between the Church and culture were blurred. To be born into the empire was to be born a Christian. Such was not the case for the first century Church. The Church of the first century saw its mission as evangelizing the "lost" people living around it. The Church of Christendom, on the other hand, saw its mission as nurturing the believers born into the empire. Evangelism happened in other parts of the world and was carried out by professionals.

Over the last five centuries or so, however, the Church's influence has narrowed. It no longer controls the shape of Western civilization. During the last several years I've had the privilege of speaking in such places as Norway, Finland, France, England, and Australia. With few exceptions, in those countries the churches sit nearly empty. The average weekly worship attendance in those countries ranges from 1 to 10 percent. In the United States weekly worship attendance holds at about 40%. However, the dominant religion in the United States is folk religion which deifies traditional American values. This civil religion retains and uses the symbols of traditional Christianity, but with the meanings changed.[12]

To be born into the empire no longer means to be born a Christian. Each generation of people is becoming increasingly secular, meaning they have little or no Christian experience. The Church does not influence their lives. They are biblically and liturgically illiterate. They have no idea what Christians are talking about. As a result, congregations can no longer assume that people have been or are being shaped by the gospel.

During my internship at Community Church of Joy I was assigned to teach the seventh grade confirmation class. We used the standard curriculum published by our Lutheran publishing house. While well written and high in quality, I quickly learned that the lessons assumed a Lutheran upbringing. The lessons built on the belief that the students had been through a Lutheran Sunday school system. Sixty percent of my students, however, came to class with little or no church experience (because their parents were new to the faith). I found that most of the students didn't know Adam from Moses or Paul from John. We had to throw out the curriculum and create our own—a program that began with the basics. We could not assume anything.

The influence of Christendom is over. Reaching new generations of secular people will require new ideas, new language, and new programs.

MOVING FROM YESTERDAY TO TOMORROW

Each generation of Christians has had to wrestle with ministry in a changing culture. The same holds true today. The challenge, however, is that change today happens more quickly. The paradigm shifts are becoming increasingly significant. Because the world keeps changing, the Church, to be effective, must respond with changes of its own. It must explore tomorrow's possibilities and discover or rediscover a new passion for ministry in this new world. That may mean reevaluating or even letting go of some of yesterday's models. For what worked yesterday will not necessarily work today. That doesn't mean we devalue the great work done in generations past. It does mean that we take today's realities seriously and continue the work in new ways.

To be effective, tomorrow-oriented churches will move from:

A focus on second generation Christians to a focus on first generation converts. A few years ago I attended a conference featuring Doug Murren, the pastor of Eastside Foursquare Church in Kirkland, Washington. During a question and answer period, Doug was asked if his church baptized infants. He responded by saying that his denomination hasn't really dealt with the issue of second generation Christians—the children of new Christians or long-time church members. As he answered, it hit me that many mainline denominations haven't fully dealt with the issue of *first* generation Christians. The denominations haven't adequately developed a theology for adult conversions.

At the risk of oversimplifying, most mainline denominations in the United States grew as a result of immigration and biology. For example, Lutherans from Norway or Germany moved to the new world and established new congregations. Through the birth of their children the church grew. Parents passed the faith along to their children who passed it along to their children and so on. Most people stayed with their own denomination. My family is a prime illustration. My grandfather was a Lutheran pastor. He and Grandma raised their three children in the Lutheran church. Those three children in turn raised their twelve children as Lutherans. And now, those of us who have our own kids are raising them in the Church. But—consistent with trends throughout the Church—not all of my grandparents' children, grandchildren, and great grandchildren still are Lutheran. Some have made their way to other denominations.

Because in many ways mainline denominations have been built on second generation Christians, the denominations have developed theologies of baptism and systems for nurture (Sunday school, confirmation, and so on) that deal with the issue of children of believers. The issue of reaching and nurturing new people, of making new converts, has not been as fully developed.

Unfortunately, many mainline churches and denominations function as if ships filled with people of their faith continue to cross the sea. They seem to believe that large families will come back in vogue. Though new immigrants are coming, they aren't necessarily Christians. And as the United States becomes increasingly secular, the growing numbers of unchurched people makes for a smaller group of second generation Christians.

In order to grow, mainline churches and denominations must refine, rediscover, or develop theologies and strategies for helping irreligious adults become responsible followers of Jesus Christ.

Being a church for insiders to being a church for seekers. Management expert Peter Drucker says that the nonprofit organization (including the church) "exists to bring about a change in individuals and society."[13] He goes on to say that "their 'product' is a cured patient, a child that learns, a young man or woman grown into a self-respecting adult; a changed human life altogether."[14] Jesus says it this way: "Go therefore and make disciples of all nations, baptizing them in the name of the Father and of the Son and of the Holy Spirit, and teaching them to obey everything that I have commanded you" (Matt. 28:19-20). According to Jesus, the business of the Church is to "make disciples," to lead people into a life-transforming relationship with him.

The purpose of the Church is mission. When Jesus talks about making disciples, he doesn't mean only nurturing those who already believe. For Jesus, making disciples means connecting with the unreached (those outside of the family of faith), leading them into a relationship with God (baptizing), and nurturing them in their faith (teaching them to obey everything that I have commanded you). Jesus' bias, or passion, as seen in his own mission and ministry, is to call sinners to himself. If churches are to be similarly passionate about making disciples, they must be transformed from congregations to mission centers.

In the Christendom Era, congregations catered only to believers. Evangelism was done overseas, beyond the borders of the empire, by professional missionaries. With the Christendom Era over, with people becoming increasingly secular, the Church must rediscover ways to reach those unfamiliar with the gospel. In our post-Christendom world, people like Ginny, mentioned in the introduction, become the priority. The need to expose her to Christ and help her grow in her discipleship sets the agenda for churches moving into tomorrow.

Having said that, for a congregation to focus on the unchurched does not mean ignoring or demeaning members. It does mean nurturing members, caring for them, and equipping them to reach out to their unchurched friends. It means intentionally instilling in them the necessary passion, vision, and skills for building a church for irreligious people—a church that leads secular people through the door of the congregation into nurture and back out into the world. Evangelism happens through members impassioned by the gospel.[15]

An emphasis on message to an emphasis on relationships. Research demonstrates that people respond best to the gospel when it's presented within the context of loving relationships. The Bible says the same thing: Andrew invited his brother Peter to meet Jesus (John 1:4042); Philip invited his friend Nathaniel to "come and see" Jesus (John 1:43-51); the Samaritan woman shared with her neighbors the new life she experienced in Jesus (John 4); the Philippian jailor told of his conversion and his family joined him in the waters of baptism (Acts 16:16-34). While the message is of vital importance, it is most effectively received in the context of trusted relationships. And the more exposure people have to the gospel, the more likely they are to stay committed. Those exposed to the gospel five to seven times before "accepting it" are highly likely to "own" it. Those with two or fewer exposures to the gospel before "buying in" are much more likely to drop out of the faith. Relationships give people holding power against forces that seek to distract them from the faith. Tomorrow-oriented congregations commit themselves to building meaningful relationships with the unchurched in order to share the gospel.

Concern for church membership to concern for Christian discipleship. Congregations often measure their health by the number of people on the rolls. But congregations are realizing that church membership has little to do with active discipleship. New measures of discipleship center on participation: worship attendance, giving, commitment to growth, involvement in ministry, and so on. Churches of tomorrow will focus more on the process of evangelism than on simply recruiting members. They will concentrate on moving people from unbelief to actively following Jesus Christ.

Growing the church to growing people. Tomorrow-oriented churches make a commitment to both. They know that churches grow when people have the opportunity to grow.

Being program-driven to being need-driven. Programs-for-the-sake-of-programs no longer cuts it in today's world. Keeping a Bible study going simply because it has "always" been offered does little to enhance ministry. Effective churches begin with the needs of people and create programs to meet those needs.

Focusing on efficiency to focusing on effectiveness. The question "Are we doing something well?" has been replaced by "Are we doing the right thing?" The question is no longer "Is the program running smoothly?" but "Is it meeting real needs?" Is the program achieving its purpose? When a program no longer meets the intended need, the church disbands it or renews it.

Commitment to a doctrinal statement to commitment to a vision. Many free agents consider doctrinal statements or institutional creeds irrelevant. Instead, they rally around a meaningful vision for the future; something bold, daring, and life-transforming; something through which they can make a difference. Creating a church for new generations means upholding exciting visions that attract people. At the same time these visions will communicate the substance of faith the church embraces.

REKINDLING THE PASSION

The world has changed. And tomorrow-oriented churches know that ministry must change as well. But they don't simply change for the sake of change. Any change they make is driven by a rekindled passion for reaching new people.

Years ago a king went hunting with some friends. While walking through the woods they noticed a group of people gathered on the river bank. As they made their way over to the river they quickly learned that a man had fallen into it. The heavy currents were dragging him toward a waterfall. They also discovered that the victim was a condemned criminal. Before anyone realized what was happening, the king dived into the river. He swam toward the man and pushed him over to a rock. Unfortunately, as the criminal hung onto the rock, the falls dragged the king to his death.

The people on the bank eventually rescued the criminal. And from that moment on his life was different. The king had died for him. Every day he received reminders of how his life had been spared. Whenever people saw him they would say, "You're the one the king died for." That sacrifice changed his life. And because of it, he went on to become a model citizen.

Tomorrow-oriented congregations passionately believe that Jesus, the King, died for all people. They believe that he can change any life, that following him is the greatest adventure on earth. And that belief shapes their understanding of mission. Through prayer and Bible study they take the time to discover who it is God wants them to be. They seek to discover God's heart, to make God's passion for lost people theirs. They seek:

- a passion that leaves behind the 99 to find the one that is lost
- a passion that tears apart an entire house to find one lost coin
- a passion that lays down one's life for a friend
- a passion that sets aside its own rights for the sake of others
- a passion that sees lost people through the eyes of Jesus
- a passion that puts the needs of the unchurched ahead of the churched
- a passion that risks letting go of certain traditions that might be barriers to reaching new people
- a passion that will do whatever it takes to invite people to discover the joy of discipleship

Tomorrow-oriented congregations find their motivation for ministry in the passion to reach new people, to get people in the door. Armed with that passion, they take whatever risks necessary to build a church for the unchurched.

DREAMSHOP

1) Think through the significant cultural, historical, and sociological events of your life. List them. How have they affected you? How have they affected life in general? How is your generation different from the one before and the one after yours? What values and beliefs are unique to your generation?
2) How do you perceive the attitude in our society toward religion in general, and Christianity specifically, has changed over the years, if at all?

3) What ministries in your church, if any, seem to be based on the assumption that people have had a churched background? What ministries, if any, grow out of the assumption that the people have had little or no Christian experience?
4) What changes might need to take place in your congregation to move from a Christendom to a post-Christendom ministry? Why?
5) Consider which of the twelve societal changes listed in this chapter are most reflected in your congregation, and in our community.
6) For each of the eight characteristics of "tomorrow," draw a continuum and put an "x" where your congregation is today. Indicate where you would like it to be in two years and in five years. What do you need to do to accomplish your goal? Begin to sketch out some plans.

The increasing secularity of society calls for a rekindled passion on the part of churches—a passion to be about the business that Jesus is about: calling irreligious people back home to God. Tomorrow-oriented churches, inspired by that passion, see their church as a mission station for those not yet reached by the gospel. The members rally around that passion and work together to create an inviting, open climate that attracts secular people. And they make their passion concrete through the development of a mission statement.

THE MISSION STATEMENT

•

mission: specific function, task, or service
that a person or group of persons
is sent or officially assigned to do.

—MERIT STUDENTS DICTIONARY

CHAPTER 2

DEFINING
YOUR MISSION

•

*Go out into the roads and lanes, and
compel people to come in, so that my
house may be filled.*

(LUKE 14:23)

Two elderly sisters went to a shopping mall about 20 miles from
their home. On the way back to their house they made a wrong
turn and lost their way. For the next two and a half days they tried
to find their home. During that time they didn't stop to ask for
help. They didn't take time to eat. And finally, they ended up stuck
in a muddy orange grove. Eventually a passerby noticed their di-
lemma and stopped to help. By that time one of the sisters had died
from exposure. The other was in critical condition. During the
investigation the police tried to retrace the sisters' journey. They
estimated that the women had driven over 200 miles trying to find
their house, which was only 20 miles away!

Many congregations, like those two sisters, have lost their way.
They lack direction. They drift aimlessly from year to year with
little or no focus. And in the process, many of them lose vitality,
passion, and even hope.

To be effective, churches, like businesses, need to know where
they're headed. They need to know what business they're in and
the kind of people they're trying to reach. In other words, they
need a road map to guide them. And that road map is the mission
statement. But before they can craft a mission statement they need

an accurate understanding of what currently drives the congregation.

What Drives Your Church?

Every congregation is impassioned about or driven by something. The following descriptions identify the forces that drive some churches:

The institution-driven church. Members of these congregations have a deep love for their church. The church has meant much to them over the course of their lives. It gave and continues to give them stability, support, and spiritual nourishment. As a result they're deeply committed and loyal. They love the church the way it is and work hard to ensure it continues its ministry.

In some cases, however, this love for the church as it is can subtly turn into a commitment to preserving the institution above all else. Because the ministry works for them, the members resist any kind of change. Maintenance—keeping things as they always have been, rather than mission—leading seekers into discipleship, shapes the ministry. The members work together, pray together, and struggle together to keep the machine well oiled. They remember better times during the Christendom Era. They believe that by going back to those times and doing it better, the ministry will once again become productive. Few, if any, newcomers make their way into leadership positions. Run by committees, institution-driven congregations seek to keep the church managed as it has been for generations.

The program-driven church. Most congregations place a high value on quality programming. They use a variety of programs as tools to reach and nurture people. Dynamic congregations continually evaluate current programming and look for new ideas to better serve their people.

In program-driven congregations, however, the focus is skewed. The program, not mission nor the needs of the people, shapes the ministry. People loyal to a particular program or programs tend to hold the power in these churches. Keeping the program alive drives the church long after the program has served its useful purpose. Lifeless, often ineffective programs like confirmation instruction or women's circles go on and on with little return. Because the program itself is sacred, revising, changing, or dropping it proves next to impossible. Even adding an alternative program for new people meets resistance. One congregation dropped its denomination's women's program because it no longer met the needs of the women. Only four women attended it regularly. The congregation replaced it with a new program that attracted 200 women to the first event. Other churches in the denomination heard about it. Instead of celebrating the success, they accused the church of pulling out of the denomination!

The tradition-driven church. Mainline congregations have a rich heritage of tradition. These traditions, tracing themselves back for hundreds of years, offer stability and a firm foundation. Certain phrases ("The Lord be with you. And also with you," "He is risen! He is risen indeed!"), styles of worship, symbols, and liturgical garb, connect us with believers of the past. Tradition keeps the church rooted while it seeks to do ministry in the present.

In some congregations, however, tradition becomes equated with the gospel. Where the institution-driven congregation focuses on maintaining the institution, the tradition-driven church sees its mission as preserving tradition for tradition's sake. Rather than translating these traditions into new forms for new generations, these congregations fight to keep the traditions as they have always been. Tradition becomes an anchor holding the church to the past rather than a rudder guiding it into the future.

> Luther advised each great church council to study the issues of faith and culture in its generation, and so must we. Some groups have complete sets of concrete, cultural practices, which they regard as almost synonymous with the gospel. Their witness to Christ is frozen into cultural forms which are irrelevant and unintelligible to most people. They become museum churches with period lifestyles, music, dress, and vocabulary. Evangelism for these believers carries all of this cultural baggage. The way to the cross is through the door of their traditions.[1]

In marketing terms, the above models fall under the "production approach."

The production approach to ministry is based on the idea that things aren't changing, that people inside and outside the congregation think and act as they always have. Based on this assumption, it makes sense to "produce" a ministry product that does not change. . . . A production orientation consists of an unchanging devotion to the *production* of the product, rather than a commitment to the mission the product is intended to support.[2]

The theology-driven church. Theology keeps the church centered in God. It shapes our understanding of God and protects us from half-truths and even untruths. Theological integrity sets the tone for dynamic mission and ministry.

Some congregations, however, shape their entire ministries around preserving theological purity. Certain words or phrases become confused with the truth. Like the tradition-driven church they resist repackaging the truth in new words or forms. Without realizing it, these churches become more intent on preserving theology than on communicating it in relevant ways to a hurting world.

The member-driven church. Caring for and nurturing members has always been of utmost importance for congregations. The Apostle Paul encourages churches to "equip the saints for the work of ministry, for building up the body of Christ, until all of us come to the unity of the faith and of the knowledge of the Son of God, to maturity, to the measure of the full stature of Christ" (Eph. 4:12-13). Through worship services, Bible studies, volunteer opportunities, and a host of other activities, congregations build up their members.

Unfortunately, in too many churches, focusing on members has led to the exclusion of ministry to the unchurched. These member-driven congregations build their entire ministries on meeting their own needs. Like the institution-driven church, maintenance takes precedence over mission. Believers or denominational loyalists take priority over unbelievers. Very few churches would admit to such an emphasis. But a quick review of their worship styles and programming tells the story.

A friend of mine recently attended a funeral at a Catholic church. Though raised in the Lutheran church, he felt lost in the Catholic service. He couldn't follow it. He noticed, however, that the Catholics had no trouble at all making their way through the service. They had been raised with it. The service was geared to them.

Similarly, many, if not most, Methodist churches use worship styles geared to Methodists. They use language Methodists understand but that outsiders might find confusing. To try to attract their "own kind," they use styles and methods to which their "own kind" can relate. Their mission, in a sense, is to reach Methodists and help them grow as Methodists.

And of course, most Lutheran congregations tailor their worship services to Lutherans. Many not raised in that tradition or in church at all find the liturgy confusing. Lutherans use Lutheran language, tell Lutheran jokes, and in some parts of the country even are known to eat Lutheran food (that is, lutefisk and lefse). By focusing on our own kind, we often times miss those who have yet to be reached.

A little girl, while out for a walk, spotted a penny on the ground. She quickly picked it up and put it in her pocket. She felt a sense of excitement as she realized the penny was hers. From that moment on she walked with her head down, keeping her eyes pealed for more treasure. During her lifetime she found 302 pennies, 24 nickels, 41 dimes, 8 quarters, 3 half dollars, and one worn out paper dollar for a grand total of $12.82. But in the process of gathering her treasure, she missed out on 35,127 sunsets, the beauty of 327 rainbows, babies growing, white clouds floating across the sky, birds flying, animals running, and the smiles of passing people.

When congregations make their members the priority, they often fail to see the unchurched all around them. Some churches say they'll get around to evangelism once the congregation has enough money. Other churches want to make sure their members have been properly trained and nurtured before turning outward. But there never seems to be enough money. The members never seemed fully prepared to reach out. The church, usually without realizing it, turns so inward it can't see anything but itself. And in part because of the insistence on doing a Christendom Era ministry, mainline denominations and congregations continue to decline. By putting the needs of members first, we exclude the millions of people who do not know Jesus as Lord and Savior.

THE MISSION-DRIVEN CHURCH

Ministering effectively in our changing, post-Christendom Era means congregations will have to reevaluate their mission. To survive and to reach the millions of irreligious people, a growing number of congregations will need to become mission-driven churches. Mission-driven congregations embrace the positives listed in the above descriptions of churches. They deeply appreciate the institution of the church. They continually create innovative, relevant programs. They draw strength from their heritage and denominational traditions. They build on good, solid theology. And they love, care for, nurture, and value their members. But mission-driven congregations differ from the above churches in one key area: their passion.

Mission-driven congregations are impassioned about reaching people who do not have a relationship with God and know Jesus as Savior. They see their purpose as connecting with irreligious people and helping them become disciples of Jesus Christ. Reaching the unchurched sets the agenda for their ministries. This happens, not to the exclusion of their members, but through their members. The members passionately believe that their church exists, not just for themselves, but for others yet to be reached. Members in these congregations feel a high degree of satisfaction because their needs are being met. But more than that they find significance in the fact that through their church they are also doing mission.

Mission-driven congregations firmly root their ministries in the gospel of Christ and his call to make disciples of all people. They do not see outreach and nurture as an either/or proposition. Instead, they see both as a part of the same journey or process—it's getting them in the door, and *more* than getting them in the door. That journey or process can be summarized as follows:

Leading people into a relationship with Christ and the Church. In mainline churches this usually happens through infant baptism and confirmation as parents bring their children to church. In an increasingly secular world, mission-driven congregations also attempt to build relationships with people who have either left the church or who have never been to church. They passionately seek to translate the substance of the gospel into new styles that will effectively communicate to new people. They don't discontinue traditions that contribute to mission. They don't stop nurturing their members. Instead, they redirect their focus. Reaching the unchurched, rather than being one facet of the ministry, becomes the driving force of the congregation. It sets the agenda for everything else the church does. Mission-driven congregations augment their traditional ministry with new worship styles, programming, language, and strategies in order to reach those outside of the faith.

Thomas Aquinas once said that to convert people we need to go over to where they're standing, take them by the hand, and guide them. We don't reach them by standing across the room and yelling at them or exhorting them to live differently. Instead, we connect with them when we go to them on their terms, speaking to them in their language. Mission-driven churches seek to lead people into a relationship with Christ and the Church by building a church geared to secular people; by sharing the gospel in language, worship styles, and ministries secular people understand.

Building them up. In many mainline congregations, nurture systems care for people from the cradle to the grave. Such systems, however, often assume that those being nurtured began the process as infants, that from birth on they have been enculturated into the church. Because they reach unchurched people, mission-driven churches find it necessary to design and add new nurture systems to the program menu for newly converted adults. Mission-driven congregations offer growth opportunities for all people, no matter where people are in their spiritual journey.

Sending them out. While managing the church is important, mission-driven congregations place a heavier emphasis on training volunteers to do the work of ministry. Rather than creating more and more committees, they train and empower people to teach, visit the sick, lead worship, care for the homeless, and so on. Mission-driven congregations intentionally equip their members to go out and share the good news of Christ with others.

Mission-driven churches trace their roots back to the Apostolic Era. They see their mission as being similar to that of the early disciples—to go out to the roads and lanes inviting people to meet Jesus. And their mission statement reflects that passion.

THE MISSION STATEMENT

The mission statement is an agreed-upon statement of purpose. It states clearly and succinctly, in writing, why the church exists and who it's trying to reach. It sets the direction of the church. It informs and shapes all decisions, goals, programs, worship styles, and the like. The mission statement serves as the rudder that guides the ship. It also provides a launching pad for new dreams.

> The mission identifies the church's uniqueness, sets it apart from other churches, strengthens its boundaries, and helps members know "who we are."[3]

The mission statement grows out of the congregation's passion. It gives that passion feet by describing specific actions the congregation will take to carry out its mission. It makes the congregation's passion intentional by answering the question: "What has God called us to do?"

Specifically, the mission statement adresses the following issues:

1) Who are we trying to reach?
2) What will reach or impress them?
3) What do we want to have happen in the lives of those we're trying to reach?
4) What do we value as a congregation? What's important to us theologically, historically, biblically, and socially?
5) Finally, given our audience and values, what is our mission, and how will we carry it out?

MISSION STATEMENT RESOURCES

In order to get at the answers to those questions, congregations can look to the following resources for guidance:

Prayer. Prayer gives birth to dynamic mission statements. Through prayer the church seeks the guidance of the Spirit. In faithful expectation congregations ask the Spirit what God wants them to do. Prayer empowers the mission statement. Without it, the mission statement becomes yet another forgotten piece of paper.

The Bible. Through the Bible God shares his heart with us. God tells us what's most important. Passages abound indicating God's

passion for reaching lost people, compassion for the poor and out-
cast, desire to reconcile the world to himself through Jesus, and so
on. Congregations serious about connecting with God's heart will
turn to the Bible for direction. Through the study of God's word
and prayer, God will lead congregations to his mission for them.

The beliefs of the congregation and the denomination. While
creeds and traditions hold little meaning for the unchurched and
can serve as barriers that keep the unchurched from exploring a
church further, they do influence the mission and personality of
congregations and denominations. They communicate what congregations believe and what they hold dear. In other words, the
forms (creeds and traditions) communicate the substance of the
faith. And the substance of faith shapes the mission of churches.

Each congregation has certain beliefs that offer guidance during
the mission statement shaping process. Such beliefs give focus to
the mission statement. For instance, congregations embracing "decision" theology will shape their mission statements differently than
those committed to a "Word and Sacrament" model of ministry.
What congregations believe and value affects their understanding
of mission and how they carry it out.

Denominational congregations also have the rich resources of
the denomination behind them. What does the history of Meth-
odism or Catholicism or any other denomination have to say about
mission today? What seem to be the current issues shaping the
mission of the denomination? How do those issues affect the mission
of the local church?

The strengths and weaknesses of the congregation. Discovering
the mission depends, in part, on the resources and gifts God has
given to the church. Some congregations have the gifts to teach
churches. Other congregations have been wired to offer effective
ministry to the discouraged and displaced. When writing the mission
statement, congregations will take time to assess what they can and
cannot do.

The ministry of other congregations in the area. One way to
determine a mission is to ask: "What needs are not currently being
met by other congregations?" Once listed, the church can begin to
dream about how they might meet one or more of those needs. For

example, maybe no other congregation offers contemporary worship. Or perhaps no other congregation offers free health advice to those who can't afford a doctor. The needs of the community help shape the mission statement.

The location of the church. A rural congregation ministers to people with somewhat different needs than does an inner city church. An inner city church differs from a suburban congregation due, in part, to the distinct needs of the community. Churches surrounded by young families face different issues than those ministering in retirement areas. The location of the church has a great deal to say about the mission of the church.

The target audience. In addition to asking, "What needs are not being met by other churches?" congregations should also ask, "What people are not currently being reached by other churches in this area?" Seniors? Baby Boomers? Baby Busters? Young marrieds? Career-minded singles? Church dropouts? The never-been-to-church population? Determining one's target audience is the key to an effective mission statement. Ultimately, the needs of the target audience will shape the style of ministry and the programs offered.

> A religious organization should not define its mission by listing the particular services it offers. Rather, it should identify the group(s) it wants to serve and the needs and interests of the group(s) that the organization will try to satisfy.[4]

For more on defining the target audience, see chapter 3.

THE CHARACTERISTICS OF A MISSION STATEMENT

The following characteristics help give life to a mission statement. A mission statement is:

Biblical. As previously mentioned, the mission statement grows out of prayer and Bible study. A solid mission statement builds on a biblical foundation.

Motivational. An effective mission statement inspires people. It ignites enthusiasm for the mission of the church. But more than ignite enthusiasm, it motivates people to go out and accomplish the mission. A well-crafted mission statement gives people a sense of ownership and pride in the church.

Dynamic. A mission-statement focuses on action. It moves the congregation toward something. It focuses on the "to do" and the "can do." Because of this action emphasis, the mission statement enables the congregation to measure its effectiveness.

Concise. In clear, specific terms, the mission statement lays out the direction of the church. By describing what the congregation will do, the mission statement subtly describes what the church will not do. For instance, Community Church of Joy targets the unchurched. It sees its mission as leading the unchurched into a relationship with Christ and the church. To carry out the mission, the congregation has developed several contemporary worship services built around the needs of secular people. Offering a highly liturgical worship service, on the other hand, is not seen as crucial to carrying out the mission. The church does not have a negative view of traditional liturgies. That particular style of worship simply does not fit with its mission. The mission statement helps the church determine what it will and will not do.

> A mission serves best when it is distinctive. A well-stated mission allows persons to make differential comparisons, allowing members and seekers to see how and why this church is different from the other churches in the community, thus helping persons to decide whether this is the church for them.[5]

Mission-oriented. The bias of this book suggests that mission (focusing on the unreached) should be at the heart of all that the church is about. Effective mission statements of the next century will focus on connecting with secular people.

Memorable. A good mission statement is easy to memorize. It captures the heart and the imagination.

MISSION STATEMENT EXAMPLES

The following two mission statements help illustrate the above characteristics:

> That all may know Jesus Christ, and become responsible members of his church, we share his love, with joy, inspired by the Holy Spirit.

In one brief sentence this congregation states its mission as: Reaching the unchurched—**that all may know Jesus Christ**—and helping them grow in the faith—**and become responsible members of his church**. The mission is carried out by all members—**we share his love, with joy, inspired by the Holy Spirit**. This mission statement enables the congregation to measures its effectiveness by the number of unchurched who join the congregation and get involved in growth and service.

> To attract and win members, develop them to Christ-like maturity, and empower them for a meaningful ministry in the church and a life of mission in the world in each stage and segment of their lives.

This congregation clearly states its purpose—to reach the unchurched and lead them into responsible discipleship.

DREAMSHOP

1) What currently drives your congregation? Who makes the decisions? Based on what?
2) What does your congregation do well? Where do most of the energies and resources of the church go? Does the flow of energies and resources reflect the true passion and calling of the congregation? If not, what needs to change, and how?
3) What beliefs does your church embrace? What message do you want to communicate to people? What traditions can be reshaped in order to be meaningful for new generations? How might this happen? What traditions, if any, cannot be changed?
4) What is your understanding of the mission of the church as described in the Bible? What business should the church be about? Is this happening in your congregation?
5) Does your church have a mission statement? Does the congregation know what it is? Does it adequately express the purpose of your congregation today?

CHAPTER 3

TARGETING
YOUR AUDIENCE

•

*The Church exists by mission as a fire
exists by burning.*

*(Emil Brunner,
twentieth-century Swiss theologian)*

A Lutheran pastor starting a new mission congregation was asked how it was going. The pastor sighed and replied, "Not too well. There aren't many Lutherans in this area."

Unfortunately, an old paradigm shaped the methodology for developing that new congregation. The course of its ministry was based on the assumption that we still live in the Christendom Era. The pastor lived under the outdated assumption that the mission of the church centers on reaching those already reached, on those already committed to our denominations. Sadly, many congregations function under the same mindset. The result: plateaued or dying churches and denominations.

Several years ago I had a discussion with an acquaintance of mine about worship and its relationship to evangelism. He openly struggled with the concept of designing worship services for the unchurched. At one point he said: "If we simply do worship with excellence, if believers worship with enthusiasm, the unchurched will come." That assumption, however, no longer holds true in a world influenced less and less by the Church. Evangelism does not happen as a by-product of an excellent ministry to believers. Dynamic worship, geared to believers, more often than not fails to capture the attention of the unchurched. Congregations making their own members the priority often find it difficult to effectively reach the unreached.

A PROFILE OF TODAY'S NON-CHURCHED PERSON

A commitment to reaching new generations of people means putting evangelism on the front burner. And that necessitates taking the time to understand the mind of unchurched people, for the unchurched person's view of faith and church differs significantly from that of churched people. So reaching secular people might require new strategies and programming.

The following general characteristics give us insights into the needs and values of secular people.

Secular people are becoming increasingly ignorant of Christianity.[1] As the church loses its influence on society, fewer and fewer people find their lives informed by Christianity. They view as unintelligible the traditions, language, and worship styles so highly valued by those of us committed to the Church. George G. Hunter III, from Asbury Theological Seminary, says secular people are not "churchbroke," meaning they don't know how to act in church.[2] They fail to understand or appreciate the meaning of the gospel. Where in apostolic times people were hostile to the gospel, today they're uninformed or even apathetic.

Secular people, though increasingly ignorant of Christianity, are highly spiritual. Surveys show that secular people perceive churches as boring, irrelevant, unfriendly, and money hungry. Some even believe that the Church lacks intelligence. George Barna reports that 91% of non-Christians find congregations insensitive to their needs.[3] But being turned off to the Church doesn't necessarily mean being turned off to God. As *Newsweek* pointed out in an article entitled "Talking to God," "In allegedly rootless, materialistic, self-centered America, there is also a hunger for a personal experience of God."[4]

Entertainment Weekly has suggested the same thing. The writer of a story on spirituality and the entertainment industry observed:

> In a year when TV airwaves are aflutter with winged spiritists, the best-seller lists are clogged with divine manuscripts and

visions of the afterlife, and gangsta rappers are elbowed aside
on the pop charts for the hushed prayers of Benedictine
monks, you don't have to look hard to find that pop culture
is going gaga for spirituality.[5]

Baby Boomers have moved into midlife. And one of the questions
now facing them as middle-aged adults is: "What am I going to do
with the second half of my life?" Their children are growing up.
Parents and even friends are beginning to die. Many have reached
the apex of their careers. As a result, questions of meaning are
becoming increasingly important. Spirituality is growing in value.
Baby Busters also hunger for meaning in life. As they stand at
the beginning of their adult lives they're asking the question, "What
am I going to do with my life, period?" The path ahead of them
seems filled with pitfalls and detours. They're having a hard time
breaking into a tight job market. Wages are down in real dollars
since the 1970s. The challenges of AIDS, the environment, and the
rising federal deficit cloud the horizon. And in the midst of all of
that, Busters want to find meaning in life.
All the signs point to a growing spiritual awareness among people
in the United States. But the spiritual awakening of the 1990s will
be very different from other great awakenings in our country's
history. For a spiritual awakening today does not necessarily mean
embracing Christianity.

> In its most popular form, the baby boom's spiritual quest will
> blend the findings of psychology with the longings of religion,
> a unique blend of science and spirituality. Look for the emer-
> gence of a religion of individualism, or spiritual therapy. . . .
> Spiritual therapy will be personal and private rather than
> institutional. . . . Its goal will not be the greater good, but to
> make boomers feel good about themselves and the legacy they
> leave behind. . . . As boomers age, the focus of their spiritual
> quest. . . . will be less about self-help and more about self-
> understanding . . . about accepting themselves, their children,
> and circumstances as they are . . .[6]

Entertainment Weekly also suggests that spirituality will not necessarily lead people to church:

> "This is not religion we're talking about," says Sydny Miner, executive editor of Simon and Schuster's trade paperback division. "What we're talking about is, 'We don't want to go back to church, but we want the security, and we want to feel like we're being taken care of.' " James Morrow (whose satirical novel *Towing Jehovah* tells of a supertanker captain ordered to haul God's body to the Arctic) agrees: "Mainstream churches no longer seem to answer people's needs. Everybody's flailing about. Some people land in the New Age sector, others turn to fundamentalist Christianity, and others turn to the self-help section and find all these books on angels."[7]

In spite of the negativity many feel toward churches, congregations can still be at the leading edge of this coming spiritual revival. To do so, however, will mean finding innovative ways to speak relevantly to these new generations of spiritual seekers.

Secular people hunger for intimacy. In an increasingly fragmented and individualistic world, people crave healthy relationships. The isolation brought on by fax machines, computers, cellular phones, and broken families leaves people crying for human contact. They also desire intimacy in their spirituality. Focusing on a relationship with Jesus can speak to and connect with that need.

Secular people lack life skills. One of the reasons people hunger for intimacy is that they seem to be increasingly at a loss as to how to build healthy relationships. At a conference I attended in Minneapolis, Lyle Schaller put his finger on the problem. He said that people today lack life skills—parenting skills, marriage skills, social skills, skills for building and maintaining new relationships, and so on. The church can help by offering gospel-centered, biblically based seminars, classes, and sermons on how to build relationships.

Secular people long for dignity. Boomers' hunger for worth and value fueled an explosion of self-help books in the 1970s and 1980s and continues to do so. The aimlessness currently seen in many Busters might trace its roots to their low self-esteem. Whatever the reason—years of put-downs, abuse, a false understanding of our roots, and so on—many struggle with their sense of dignity and value. Christianity has much to say to a broken world about our God-given worth.

Secular people are world-wise. Because we now live in an age of information, people have many options from which to choose—options in products, philosophies, and even religion. They don't buy into something simply because the ad tells them to. They don't accept Christianity because the Bible says it's true. Today's consumers evaluate their options. And often, especially when it comes to spirituality, they'll pick and choose what appeals to them the most. Then they'll blend those choices into a self-made religion.

Reaching secular people for Christ means finding new ways to help them understand the uniqueness of the gospel. That's why a strong emphasis on Jesus is so important. Every religion believes in God in some way. Jesus sets Christianity apart. And, as stated above, Jesus provides the focal point for intimacy with God.

PERSONALIZING SECULAR PEOPLE

Having painted a portrait of secular people in broad strokes, mission-driven churches then seek to personalize that picture. Each community and group is unique. Irreligious people in rural communities might view life somewhat differently than their counterparts in the suburbs. Northerners hold different attitudes than those in the south. The generations born before World War II see life from one perspective, and those born after the war look at it from another. Consequently, each mission-driven church must develop its own profile of the person it wants to target, a profile of the secular person in its community.

Community Church of Joy, inspired by Saddleback Valley Church in Mission Viejo, California, has developed a profile of the people it wants to reach.[8] Joy, an Evangelical Lutheran Church in America congregation, is located in Glendale, Arizona, a suburb of Phoenix. Glendale is a middle class community consisting of a large proportion of Baby Boomers. However, Sun City, a retirement community, sits next door to Glendale. The close proximity of Joy to Sun City creates an interesting mix of worship attenders.

Joy's target audience:

- is between 25 and 47 years of age. Many who participate at Joy are older or younger than that target age. Gearing ministry to that particular age group, however, helps Joy focus the ministry. The church learns as much as it can about the values, beliefs, and lifestyles of its target audience in order to reach some of them.

Targeting an audience is an important step in defining the mission of the congregation. It puts a human face on the ministry's purpose. Once a congregation settles on its audience, it can use the music, language, and styles that appeal to those people. Others, who find some commonality with the target group, will also be reached. However, trying to please everyone ultimately wins no one.

A radio station that plays a country-western song followed by a heavy metal band followed by a piano concerto followed by hip hop will alienate everyone. Radio stations targeting a certain audience and musical preference will reach many in that group. The truth is, every congregation targets a particular audience. The music used, for example, proves it. Many have simply not defined their audience.

- listens primarily to contemporary music. Most people today do not listen to organ music or hymns on their radios. In Phoenix the top music formats are country-western and adult contemporary. Classical music stations find it very difficult to maintain an audience at all. Joy uses contemporary and country music to attract those it wants to reach.

> Using resonant music or lyrics in boomer communications, when appropriate, may prompt boomers to attend more closely to your message.[9]

Music is the story-telling vehicle of today's generations. Like parables, music emotionalizes the message and moves it to the heart. Choosing the right style of music will prove crucial in reaching and communicating with the target audience.

- prefers the casual and informal over the formal. In Phoenix, people like to dress down, especially on the weekends. Unchurched people in particular don't want to have to dress up to go to church. People come to Joy wearing shorts, polo shirts, dresses, coats and ties, or whatever they might find comfortable. The overwhelming majority, however, dress very casually. The worship leaders and pastors reflect that casual feel in the way they dress. They avoid liturgical robes, which can be a barrier for this particular target audience. Valuing the casual also permeates the feel or climate of the service. A relational, casual (not sloppy) atmosphere takes priority over a more formal, traditional one.

In some cultures, where people dress down all week long, they look forward to dressing up on Sundays, and the service needs to be somewhat more formal, too. Each congregation should assess its own culture and target audience and respond appropriately.

- prefers large groups rather than small groups when being introduced to the church. Most people, when first visiting a congregation, look for a large group experience. They value anonymity. They simply want to check out the church. Many newcomers find small groups too intimate for an initial introduction. So Joy puts a great deal of effort into making worship (the large group) as inviting and seeker-friendly as possible. Small groups, while occasionally evangelistic, function as growth opportunities for those already committed to the church.
- tends to be overextended financially. Young to middle-age, middle-class families find their money stretched in many directions: buying a home, raising children, sending them off to college, paying taxes, and so on. Insensitive money appeals will turn them off.
- has little familiarity with the Bible, religious language, or church tradition. Joy takes this seriously in the way that it designs its worship experiences. For example, instead of identifying "the Epistle" or "the Gospel," Joy refers to "the Bible reading." The music staff carefully chooses contemporary forms of music (that is, pop or country) that speak about a relationship with God in lyrics accessible to nonreligiously trained people. Instead of using words like *justification* or *redemption,* the pastors talk about "unconditional acceptance" or about "becoming friends with God." (For more on this, see chapter 4).
- is open to a good, relevant church. Barna Research found that one out of four unchurched people would willingly attend a

church service if invited by a friend.[10] Joy seeks to build a church to which its members feel comfortable inviting others. In fact, 81% of Joy's members invite at least one friend to church each year. The members know that their friends will hear dynamic, relevant music. They know that their friends will hear sermons that deal with daily life. They know that their friends will be treated as honored guests, that they will not be embarrassed or stand out. They know that their friends will understand the service, and more importantly, that they will understand what's being said about the Savior. (Again, for more information see chapter 4).

DISCOVERING YOUR TARGET AUDIENCE

In order to determine the characteristics of the target audience several ideas might prove helpful:

1) The chamber of commerce, libraries, or local newspapers often have statistics available detailing life in the community. The information includes: the different age groups in the community, the average income, professions, and so on. This information can be invaluable.
2) Some denomination headquarters provide demographics for specific communities.
3) Businesses that have recently located in the area might be willing to share their demographic research.
4) Discovering your "potential congregation" can also help personalize the target audience. The potential congregation consists of the members' unchurched friends, neighbors, business associates, and family who live within reasonable driving distance of the church but who do not currently attend church.

Discovering the potential congregation can be a strong motivator for the church family. Congregation members gather in small groups and begin to talk about their unchurched family and friends. The discussion focuses on the concerns and needs of these potential members, asking why they don't come to church and what might encourage them to come.

Out of such small group experiences your congregation might learn that five women within the potential congregation have recently been widowed. Someone might suggest that the church consider offering a grief support group targeted to them and that need.

Maybe several men have been identified who share an interest in softball. Someone might then suggest developing teams consisting of a mix of these potential members and current members of the church.

The potential congregation exercise has many benefits. It gets members thinking about their unchurched friends and family members. It forces them to evaluate the church—its worship and programming—from the perspective of secular people. It gets them involved in dreaming new dreams. And finally, it helps them buy into a mission-driven perspective.

5) Certainly, before starting any kind of ministry for the unchurched, we'll want to listen to them. As believers we may not always accurately read their needs and concerns. Often, as I share workshops on the perceptions unchurched Baby Boomers and Baby Busters have of the Church, pastors challenge some of my assumptions. They say that they have Boomers and Busters who don't think at all like the people I'm talking about. But as the discussion continues, it becomes apparent that the Boomers and Busters in their churches have been enculturated by the church. Being raised in the church, these Boomers and Busters have a church mindset. To reach the unchurched, we need to view the church and life through their eyes.

Asking unchurched friends, neighbors, or coworkers about their views of the church can be very informative. Most people, if asked in the right way, are more than willing to talk about their impressions of the church. At Joy, I assigned one of my evangelism classes the task of talking to their unchurched friends about church. They opened the door of conversation by saying, "I'm doing an assignment for my church. We're trying to find out how our church can better serve the needs of the community. Do you mind if I get your opinion?" They then asked questions similar to the following: "Why do you think most people stay away from the church?" and "What can the church do to improve its image?" If, during the conversation, the respondents said they felt that worship was boring, the questioner might ask, "What can the church do to make its worship more exciting?"

Dreamshop: Crafting the Mission Statement

The following process might help you write a mission statement:

1) Begin with prayer asking what God wants your congregation to do.
2) Assign an individual or a committee to research the community through the library, chamber of commerce, and so on.
3) Ask some unchurched friends about their views of the church.
4) Set a date for doing the potential congregation exercise.
5) Compile the results from questions 2-4 and answer the following questions:

   - What is our biblical understanding of mission?
   - Who are we currently reaching? What is the average age of our community? What is the average age of our church? How do the two compare? In general, does our congregation reflect the community?
   - Who would we like to reach?
   - What do we do well as a church? What would we like to improve?
   - What needs are not being met by other churches in our community? What people are not being reached? What are the characteristics of this target audience (their values, attitudes, beliefs, musical tastes, view of church, and so on)?
   - What will reach them? What activities, styles of worship, or programs might attract them? Develop a profile of the target audience.

6) Funnel the information into written answers to these questions: Who are we? What is our purpose? (That is, what does God expect us to do? Why do we exist?) Who is our target audience? How will we reach them?
7) Distill those answers into one or two sentences, which become your mission statement. Keep in mind the mission statement characteristics from chapter 2 as you mold and shape it.
8) Try it on for awhile. Live with it. Pray about it. And finally, commit to it.

You've probably heard it said that if we don't know where we're headed, any road will take us there. Unfortunately, most of those roads lead to dead ends. Effective churches, through the guidance of the Spirit, choose their road and focus their ministry. They chart the course and steer the bus toward the mission of transformation. And to effectively carry out their mission they learn to connect with secular people.

CHAPTER 4

CONNECTING WITH SECULAR PEOPLE

•

I tell you, there will be more joy in heaven over one sinner who repents than over ninety-nine righteous persons who need no repentance.

(LUKE 15:7)

A "Doonesbury" cartoon pictures a mom and dad sitting on the sofa having a heart to heart talk with their son, Alex. Dad begins the conversation by saying, "Alex, honey, mom and I have been talking, and we've decided it's time to start attending church as a family."

"Church?" responds a stunned Alex. "Church is boring."

"Well, we thought you might say that," says dad.

"Didn't *you* think church was boring when you were a kid?" asks Alex.

"Well, sure, I hated going," admits dad. "But church was good for me, so my parents made me stick it out. You may end up hating church, too, but you have to come by that feeling honestly. You have to put in the pew time, like mom and I did."

"Oh." After a long pause Alex asks, "What if I like it?"

Caught off guard dad replies, "Like it? What do you mean?"

To which mom says, "We'll cross that bridge when we get there, honey."[1]

That "Doonesbury" cartoon captures the good news and the bad news when it comes to reaching secular people. The good news: Parents seem eager to involve their children in some kind of religious environment. The bad news: A large number of unchurched people perceive the church as boring. In order to take advantage of the good news, congregations will have to overcome the bad news. They will have to find ways to change the perception the irreligious have of church by removing several barriers.

Barriers to Reaching the Irreligious

Barrier #1—The perception that worship is boring. A few years ago I watched an episode of a short-lived television program called, "American Dreamer." The show focused on a recently widowed dad trying to raise his two children in a rural town. This particular episode dealt with the father's religious roots. Since the death of his wife, he hadn't been to church. But then he met and became friends with the new Episcopal priest in town. Since he admired the priest he decided that maybe he should give church another try. So that night he proudly announced to his children that they would all be going to church on Sunday. Both of the kids looked at him in horror and said, "Church? Why do we have to go to church? What did we do wrong?"

For many secular people church is the last place they want to be. The reason: They perceive worship to be boring, lifeless, and slow. Most currently unchurched Boomers attended church as children. As they look back on those years they remember lethargic, dull services. They recall the religiosity and the unintelligibility of the language. Their perception of the church (which, unfortunately, is too often accurate) keeps them away.

Barrier #2—The perception that the church is unfriendly. My family and I are big Disney fans. Two or three times a year we run over to Disneyland to have some fun. It helps us relax and let go of some of the stress of life. Part of the allure of Disneyland for us is the way the employees make us feel. We always feel like honored guests. The "cast," as Disney calls them, go out of their way to create a warm, homey environment. They always put the needs of their guests first.

During a recent summer vacation we visited a theme park in Virginia. While we enjoyed our time there, we knew immediately that we weren't in a Disney park. We didn't experience the same kind of care and hospitality. One experience in particular provided an insight.

We were waiting for the train to take us around the park. As we waited, my wife and I observed how the conductors talked with each other and ignored the guests. At Disney, the conductors make it a point to engage their guests in conversation. My wife said, "It's kind of like the church. It's so easy for us to talk to each other and, without realizing it, ignore new people."

Unfortunately, she's right. Often, because we greet people we know, we believe our congregation is friendly. But without realizing it, we might be creating an unfriendly church by not intentionally welcoming new people. Many congregations lack any kind of formal guest relations system—a welcome center, well-trained hosts and hostesses, and so on. Members assume everyone knows their way around the church grounds. Few if any signs direct visitors to the sanctuary, offices, restrooms, or the nursery. When visitors enter such an atmosphere, they feel subtly unwelcome, devalued, and even unwanted.

A cowboy visited church for the first time in his life. After the experience he told a friend all about it. He said, "I rode up on my horse and tied it up by a tree in the corral."

The friend said, "You don't mean corral; you mean parking lot."

"I don't know, maybe that is what they called it," he said. "Then I went in through the main gate."

"You don't mean the main gate; you mean the front door of the church."

"Well, anyway, a couple of fellows took me down the long chute."

"You don't mean the long chute; you mean the center aisle."

"I guess that is what they called it. Then they put me in one of those little box stalls."

"You don't mean a box stall; you mean a pew!"

"Oh, yes! Now I remember!" said the cowboy, "That's what the lady said when I sat down beside her!"

George Hunter, as previously noted, would say that that cowboy and visitors like him are "not churchbroke"; they do not understand the culture of the church. Yet many congregations, by their lack of a guest relations system, assume that only the churchbroke will attend.

Barrier #3—Irrelevant preaching. Understandably, irreligious people find the gospel difficult to comprehend. Christianity has language, beliefs, and traditions that take time to assimilate and appreciate. However, boring or unimaginative preaching that makes the gospel even more difficult to grasp turns people away. Overly long messages lacking daily relevance, smacking of judgmentalism, or pushing a certain agenda of the denomination, lose guests. When asked what would attract them to church, the unchurched ranked better preaching as number one.[2]

STAYING AWAY BUT STILL OPEN

In spite of the barriers, many of the unchurched remain open to a good, relevant congregation. One-half of all Baby Boomer dropouts admit to having looked at congregations they might attend.[3] Seventy-one percent rate the chances of getting involved in a church as very high.[4] They'll return if they find a church they like. Several factors lie behind their interest in looking for a church. (Notice how these reasons for considering church relate to the characteristics of secular people listed in chapter 3.)

Family concerns. Many unchurched people desire religious training for their children. Ginny, mentioned in the introduction, provides such an example. When her daughter asked faith questions Ginny couldn't answer, Ginny decided to find a church. A *Newsweek* cover story captured this phenomenon.[5] The story focused on Boomer families returning to church out of concern for the religious welfare of their children. Many parents today feel frustrated. They want to raise healthy children but don't know how. Some believe the church and/or religious training might help. Churches can attract many unchurched parents by designing helpful parenting seminars and classes. Members will find such opportunities an excellent "excuse" for inviting their unchurched friends to church.

The search for a meaningful philosophy of life. Boomers, driven by a search for meaning, might find the search leading them to church. Being highly inner-driven, they long to feel fulfilled. As they try to make sense out of life, faith and church takes on greater importance. Busters also long for a meaningful philosophy of life. Much in their lives seems "busted." So they crave something that will help them put their lives back together.

Midlife concerns. When people move into midlife, as Boomers are now doing, they begin to reevaluate life. Questions of mortality, meaning, and spirituality take on a new sense of urgency. Such a transition provides congregations yet another opportunity to reach out to those uncommitted to the church.

The need to belong. Many people feel lonely and alienated. They long for intimacy. Free agents can only depend on themselves for so long before their God-given desire for relationships finally wins out. Busters, feeling alienated from family and society, hunger for intimacy with their peers. Churches should be experts in building relationships. Friends inviting friends into relationships at church builds congregations and disciples.

The search for values. When it comes to values, a growing number of free agents feel confused. Somewhere along the path of self-centered living they lost their moral compass. So as they try to create new values, those values take on a self-centered quality.

> . . . moral issues have shifted away from those spelled out by the Ten Commandments, which banned work on the Sabbath, taking the name of the Lord in vain, adultery, and the longing for material goods. Instead, the new moral guidelines seek to control behavior that has the potential of harming individual free agents and their families. . . . At the core of moral values of free agents is self-interest. The issues that galvanize them are those that threaten them personally: smokers beside them in a restaurant; drunk drivers on the road; . . . boys with unknown HIV status dating their daughters . . .[6]

Occasionally, free agents find that their self-centered values conflict with their family and community obligations. As a result they feel lost. Many see the church as a place for values-guidance. A sensitive friend, in partnership with a sensitive congregation, might help meet that need.

OVERCOMING THE BARRIERS

Many unchurched people remain open to church. To draw them in, however, will mean overcoming the barriers that currently keep them out.

Two thousand years ago God, in the person of Jesus, entered a world of barriers—barriers erected by the religious leaders of the day. These barriers kept people out. The rules, liturgies, language, and piety made God inaccessible to all but the religiously trained. The religious leaders essentially closed the doors to "sinners and tax collectors"—to anyone who was not like them. Their attitude was, "Come to us on our terms or don't come at all."

Jesus came to break through all of that. He came to remove the barriers that keep people from a relationship with God. Driven by his passion to reach lost people, he came to open the door so that all might enter. He did so by laying aside his rights and privileges as God in order to take the form of a servant (Phil. 2:5-11). He met people at their level. He put their needs ahead of his own. He treated people with respect. To the horror of the religious, he befriended the nonreligious. He didn't demand that they act or believe a certain way before he would speak with them. He didn't expect them to understand certain religious rites before he accepted them. Instead, he loved and accepted them unconditionally. He connected with them. He spoke in their language. He told stories that dealt with their lives. He met their needs. He made the kingdom of God accessible to them. He invited them into a relationship with himself, a relationship of forgiveness and grace.

God's strategy for reaching people, for overcoming the barriers that keep people out, was to become incarnate in the person of Jesus. In a very real sense, God—in order to understand us, identify with us, and reach us—became the "customer" he wanted to reach (Heb. 2:14-18). The Word became flesh (John 1:14).

That strategy continues to hold true today. Jesus is still impassioned about reaching lost people. And he calls the Church to be the vehicle through which he will find them. He invites the Church to understand and identify with lost people. He calls the Church to reach out to the unchurched on their terms and build a relationship with them, a relationship of unconditional love and acceptance, a relationship that will point them to God. In other words, he encourages congregations to follow his strategy: to remove the barriers that keep people from hearing about God's love and to create an environment that encourages anyone and everyone to enter regardless of their religious background.

My dad recently met a man in the waiting room of a hospital. They had exchanged stories about their children and grandchildren when the conversation turned to church. The man said he was attending a Lutheran church not far from the hospital. My dad responded by saying that he attended Community Church of Joy. He also mentioned that his son was one of the pastors.

The man said, "One of my kids goes there. That church isn't really Lutheran."

My dad replied, "Yes, they're Lutheran. Their style of worship may be different, but their theology is Lutheran. Their sermons are Lutheran."

The man said, "No, they're not really Lutheran. They let anyone in!"

Exactly!

The following keys can help congregations remove the barriers so that secular people can hear about Jesus.

Create a safe environment. Unchurched guests usually feel uptight and apprehensive when visiting a church for the first time. They don't know what to expect. Creating a visitor-friendly atmosphere helps them relax enough to actually focus on the worship service. Congregations create a safe, welcoming environment in several ways:

- by respecting a guest's desire for anonymity. Many people stay away from church because they don't want to stand out or be embarrassed. Lee Strobel, a formerly unchurched person, knows firsthand the need for anonymity. He writes:

  > Studies show that no matter how well-intentioned the congregation, most church visitors don't want to be identified during the service. What's more, a majority don't want to wear name tags or have anyone visit them in the home the following week.[7]

Unchurched guests certainly want to feel welcomed. They simply don't want to be singled out. A pleasant greeting and handshake at the church door can disarm them. A general welcome to all guests during the service (without making them stand) affirms their presence without violating their space. Sending them a letter or following up with a phone call might be appropriate in some communities. Home visits, with rare exceptions, make seekers uncomfortable. It puts them on the defensive by causing them to feel out of control on their own turf. Many see home visits as an invasion of privacy.

Several years ago I visited a congregation and made the "mistake" of signing the guest card. The next day, while I was watching Monday night football, the door bell rang. Three very nice people from the church stood at the door—uninvited. We had an extremely pleasant conversation. I told them I was studying for the ministry and already had a church home. However, they still had to make their presentation. Again, they were nice people, but they had invaded my turf, my privacy, and my football game. That kind of well-intentioned action can actually serve as an annoyance that alienates first time unchurched guests.

- by transforming members into hosts and hostesses. One congregation developed a simple process for helping their members warmly welcome guests. They call it **The Smile Strategy.** The strategy consists of five easy behaviors for caring for people:

   Smile—A smile quickly warms people up and draws them into a relationship. Smiles disarm people.

   Meaningful touch—In today's high tech world people crave a friendly handshake or pat on the back. Studies suggest that touch quickly creates a relationship.

   Inviting attitude—Being polite and courteous shows we value people.

   Listen—Listening brings honor to people. It lets them know we care.

   Eye contact—Body language experts say that by holding eye contact with someone for two seconds or more, we instantly build rapport with her or him.

Mission-driven churches find creative ways to love and care for their guests without threatening them.

- by making the buildings and property accessible. Placing signs throughout the church property helps those new to the church easily find their way around. Having a welcome booth where guests can ask questions further enhances accessibility. Lyle

Schaller said of one church: "The threshold for getting in is low. Anyone can come. It's safe here. But the risk of entering is high. For there's a good chance your life will be transformed." Mission-driven congregations excel in creating a safe environment, an environment in which the unchurched (and the current members) can experience the transforming love of Christ at their own pace.

Focus on their needs. Irrelevance keeps people away from the church. Showing them that the gospel speaks to their daily needs might encourage them to come back to hear more—and maybe even to get involved. Classes and messages dealing with family, finances, divorce recovery, emotional health, jobs, stress, and so on let the unchurched know that the congregation cares about them. It shows them that the gospel still holds meaning in today's world.

Offer choices. Boomers and Busters grew up with choices—from cable TV to different kinds of sodas. They expect choices in a church as well. They want a menu of opportunities for their children, their friends, and themselves. For example, one worship style no longer fits all, so it might be wise to use two or more styles of worship—to give people choices. By providing options, then, one congregation can gather a body of believers made up of many kinds of people.

Update worship. Recently a young man called our church office to discuss the spiritual hunger in his life. He said that he wanted to "meet Jesus." However, he shied away from coming to worship because he feared he might be confused by the service. He hadn't been to church since childhood and thought he would no longer understand the worship service. One of our pastors assured him that he would find our worship services relevant, inviting, and easy to follow. He came to our Saturday night worship service. He enjoyed it so much that he came back the next day for our Sunday services. And that afternoon, he attended our new member seminar and joined the church.

Many secular people find traditional forms of worship intimidating, largely because they don't understand them. Most mainline services have been written for people raised in the church. Churched people understand them, value them, and enjoy them. Much of that joy, however, is lost on newcomers because they have not been enculturated in the church. And what people don't understand, they quickly turn off.

Adding a service in a style that will be familiar and comfortable to the people in your community—perhaps a contemporary or country service—will enable a congregation more effectively to reach the unreached. Using the kind of music secular people listen to will attract them and speak to them, enabling them to hear the gospel. Including a drama or video clips will help them visualize the message. In other words, offering new forms of worship, forms geared to secular people, creates an inviting atmosphere. That atmosphere allows the unchurched to understand the Savior without first having to understand the service. It makes the gospel accessible to them.

Martin Luther himself encouraged three different kinds of worship experiences:

> Now there are three kinds of divine service or mass. The first is the one in Latin which we published earlier under the title *Formula Missae*. It is not my intention to abrogate or to change this service. It shall not be affected in the form which we have followed so far; but we shall continue to use it when or where we are pleased or prompted to do so. For in no wise would I want to discontinue the service in the Latin language, because the young are my chief concern. . . . The second is the *German Mass and Order of Service,* which should be arranged for the sake of the unlearned lay folk and with which we are now concerned. These two orders of service must be used publicly, in the churches, for all the people, among whom are many who do not believe and are not yet Christian. . . . The gospel must be publically preached [to such people] to move them to believe and become Christians. . . . The third kind of service should be a truly evangelical order and should not be held in a public place for all sorts of people. But those who want to be Christians in earnest and who profess the gospel with hand and mouth should sign their names and meet alone in a house somewhere to pray, to read, to baptize, to receive the sacrament, and to do other Christian works. . . .[8]

In today's world, Luther's *Formula Missae* represents traditional, liturgical worship services valued by so many raised in mainline churches. The *German Mass and Order of Service* equals a contemporary, seeker-oriented service, geared to the unchurched or "unlearned lay folk." The private service can be lived out in small groups, midweek worship services, or even family devotions. The point is, mission-driven congregations value all three. But they take mission seriously by gearing at least one service to those yet to be captured by the gospel.

Billy Graham tells the story of a woman who married a man against the strong protest of her parents. After the wedding the couple moved far away, alienating the bride from her parents. The husband turned out to be totally irresponsible and unfaithful. Within a few years he died, leaving his wife and little son penniless. In desperation the young widow scratched out a miserable living. The only real moments of joy for mother and son came when she held him in her lap and told him about her father's home. She would speak of the rich, green lawn and the beautiful trees. She would tell of the love of her parents and of the security she felt at home. Though the little boy had never seen his grandpa's house, he, along with his mom, longed to go home. One day the woman received a letter. Recognizing the handwriting she quickly tore open the envelope. In it she found a check along with a note containing two simple words: Come home!

Many secular people long to "come home." They yearn for a place where they can find meaning in life, a place where their hurts can be healed, a place where their hopes can be restored. Through worship God invites the world to come home—home to unconditional love, acceptance, and forgiveness. A warm, loving, dynamic worship service might help lead some of the lost back home to the church and the Creator.

Offer visitor-friendly sermons. Most sermons, understandably so, focus on the needs of believers. Pastors have been trained to speak to that audience. Geared to churched people, the messages assume that the listeners have biblical training and a Christian background. However, inside jokes, religious language, and vague Bible references serve only to confuse the unchurched guest.

> Evangelical Christians may as well be preaching in a foreign language, as most people are unable to define favorite evangelical terms such as the "Great Commission," "John 3:16," or

the "Gospel," according to a survey by the Barna Research
Group. The study showed that 86 percent of those surveyed
did not even try to guess the meaning of the Great
Commission. . . . Only 9 percent answered correctly. In their
understanding of the term "evangelical," . . . 66 percent had
no idea what the term meant. Eighteen percent answered
correctly. Sixty-five percent of the general population did not
know John 3:16. Thirty-three percent of the respondents
asked for the meaning of the Gospel—the "good news" of
salvation through Jesus—believed that the word was synon-
ymous with the Bible, with only 37 percent offering even a
remotely correct answer.[9]

A young wife, wishing to announce the birth of her first child,
sent the following telegram to a friend: "Isaiah 9:6." (The passage
reads, "For unto us a child is born, unto us a son is given.") The
friend, not familiar with the Bible, said to her husband, "Margaret
evidently had a nine-pound-six-ounce boy. But why on earth did
she name him Isaiah?"

Most irreligious people visit church with little if any knowledge
of Christianity. They appreciate congregations sensitive enough to
start at their level, creating messages aimed at them. They don't
necessarily want to know if the gospel is true. They want to know
if it's relevant—if it has anything to say to them about life as they
live it. Preaching on family, careers, failure, dealing with the mun-
dane, mid-life crisis, and so on will grab their attention. As they see
how the gospel applies to their lives, it will capture them and
change them.

Using language the unchurched understand is also important.
Secular Boomers, in particular, tend to use psychological language
when talking about spiritual matters. Visitor-friendly preaching
seeks meaningful ways to use that language to help people connect
with the gospel. (For more on worship and preaching please see
the author's book, *A Community of Joy: How to Create Contemporary
Worship*, Abingdon Press, 1994.)

Excel in excellence. People today expect excellence. They see
it all around them. They strive for it in their jobs. They look for it
in the products they buy. They value it in the church as well. Sloppy,

poorly planned services will lose them. Excellence in church will surprise them.

Mission-driven congregations use the best worship leaders and singers available. They seek out those with visitor-friendly voices— the kinds of voices people might hear when they listen to their favorite radio station. They recruit the best teachers possible. They keep up the property—making sure everything is clean and groomed. Mission-driven churches, inspired by the God of excellence, seek excellence in their ministries to the unchurched.

Hold up a vision. Unchurched people want to make a difference in the world. They rally around people and organizations with an inspired vision. Congregations on the move—those driven by the desire to change the world through the gospel—attract vision-minded people. They do so by offering myriads of opportunities that get people involved with the community. They instill in people a passion for mission through sermons, classes, mission seminars, and video presentations. They continually remind people of and show them the difference they can make through the church.

DREAMSHOP

1) What barriers might exist in your church that make it difficult for visitors to feel welcomed or included? What does your guest relations ministry consist of? What might you do to improve it?

2) Look at the worship service through the eyes of first time unchurched guests. What might they be thinking or feeling? What might you do to make the service more visitor-friendly?

3) Evaluate the sermons from the perspective of a newcomer. Look at the topics addressed, the language used, the relevance to everyday life, and the applicability. How might the sermons be more visitor-friendly? What topics might the sermons deal with in order to accomplish this goal?

4) Evaluate the quality of the ministry. View the grounds, the nursery, the restrooms, the paint job, and so on, as a guest. What needs to be done to give the property a sense of excellence? Who will do it? Evaluate the quality of worship and programming. Rate it on a scale of 1-10 with 10 being the highest. What can you do to move your quality closer to a 10?[10]

5) What kind of vision do you offer people? What kinds of opportunities do you currently offer that enable people to make a difference? What opportunities could you offer?

Mission-oriented churches take seriously the call to connect with irreligious people. They build their ministries around offering opportunities in which secular people can:

- experience unconditional acceptance and forgiveness
- enjoy healthy, nonjudgmental, caring relationships
- receive mental, emotional, and physical healing
- see themselves as God created them to be
- discover a brand new future
- hear about Jesus in relevant, intelligent, down-to-earth, heart-grabbing terms
- participate in life-changing mission opportunities with other believers.

In other words, they attempt to communicate the gospel in ways that speak to the unchurched. They do so with the hope of leading seekers into a life-transforming relationship with Jesus Christ and his Church. And once they get the unchurched in the door, mission-driven congregations focus on how to move them into active discipleship. To do that, they create a strategy.

BUILDING BLOCK #3

THE STRATEGY

•

strategy: plan or device designed to achieve
a specific goal or advantage.
—MERIT STUDENTS DICTIONARY

BUILDING BLOCK #4

THE PROCESS

•

process: a continuing development involving many
changes;
a particular method of doing something,
generally involving a number of steps or operations.
—NEW WORLD DICTIONARY

CHAPTER 5

MORE THAN GETTING THEM IN THE DOOR

•

I am confident of this, that the one who began a good work among you will bring it to completion by the day of Jesus Christ. . . . Therefore, my beloved, just as you have always obeyed me, not only in my presence, but much more now in my absence, work out your own salvation with fear and trembling; for it is God who is at work in you, enabling you both to will and to work for his good pleasure.

(PHILIPPIANS 1:6; 2:12-13)

A few years ago the Search Institute, an organization that conducts research on children, youth, and families, released a report entitled, "Effective Christian Education: A National Study of Protestant Congregations—A Summary Report on Faith, Loyalty, and Congregational Life." The report focused on the faith maturity of church members and clergy from five mainline denominations (Christian Church—Disciples of Christ; Evangelical Lutheran Church in America; Presbyterian Church [U.S.A.]; United Church of Christ; United Methodist Church). As a point of comparison they also included the Southern Baptist Convention. Its findings were not encouraging for mainline churches:

> Only a minority of Protestant adults evidence the kind of integrated, vibrant, and life-encompassing faith congregations

seek to develop. For most adults, faith is underdeveloped, lacking some of the key elements necessary for faith and maturity.[1]

. . . it is apparent that for many adults faith is not well formed. For more than two-thirds of adults, faith lacks a strong vertical component, a strong horizontal component, or both. This finding presents congregations with an enormous challenge. And the challenge is even greater in their ministry to men, for whom a fully integrated faith maturity is relatively uncommon.[2]

The Evangelical Lutheran Church in America, a denomination rich in heritage and liturgical worship, finished last in faith maturity. According to the Search study, 47% of adult Lutherans fall into the underdeveloped faith category. Twenty-four percent have an integrated faith. In comparison, the survey shows 23% of Southern Baptist adults in the underdeveloped faith category and 49% in the integrated faith column.[3] Though the study does not draw this conclusion, the results suggest that heritage and worship style do not in and of themselves produce responsible disciples. Worship, whether liturgical or contemporary, even though done with excellence and integrity, does not necessarily lead to maturity. Being a part of a denomination rich in tradition does not automatically result in spiritual growth. Evangelism means more than simply getting people in the door. As the Search study points out, faith maturity grows out of an effective education process.[4] Excellent worship supported by an intentional, dynamic education program helps congregations develop responsible followers of Christ. Unfortunately, the report uncovered troubled education programs in the five mainline denominations studied. Its conclusion:

> Christian education in a majority of congregations is a tired enterprise in need of reform. Often out-of-touch with adult and adolescent needs, it experiences increasing difficulty in finding and motivating volunteers, faces general disinterest among its "clients," and employs models and procedures that have changed little over time.[5]

Every congregation wants to see its people grow. As the Search Institute study suggests, however, a commitment to nurturing people may mean rethinking the structures, strategies, and education programs currently being used. This is especially true if the church wants to reach and nurture secular people. The rest of this chapter, along with chapter six and appendix A, looks at the three components of an effective education program in a mission-driven church: the strategy (the plan for carrying out the mission); the process (the pathway to growth); and the disciple profile (the content of growth).

THROUGH THE DOOR AND INTO DISCIPLESHIP

Congregations passionate about reaching people and helping them grow in their relationship with God design a strategy to make it happen. Where the mission statement answers the question, "What has God called us to do?" the strategy takes the next step by answering the question, "How will we carry out the mission?" The strategy provides an overview of the church's plan for bringing people in (connecting with secular people), building them up, and sending them out. It focuses on moving people into involvement and growth. For when it comes to growing people, the issue is not so much membership but participation.

THREE STRATEGIES

Strategy #1—The baseball diamond. Community Church of Joy uses the baseball diamond to illustrate its strategy. The object of baseball is to get runners on base with the intent of getting them home. Mission-driven churches see their purpose as helping seekers come home to a vibrant, growing faith.

- First Base—Outreach. Discipleship begins by getting irreligious people in the door, or onto first base. A **front-door** strategy uses the weekend worship service as the primary tool for attracting the unchurched. Worship is seen as a large open funnel that moves people into growth and mission opportunities.

Many congregations find it difficult to move immediately to a front-door strategy. They lack the people power or other resources to restructure their services or to create new ones. In such cases a **side-door** strategy might be appropriate. Side-door strategies use smaller events to funnel people into worship, the large event. These strategies turn the funnel upside down. Side-door opportunities might include: seminars on marriage, divorce recovery, finances, or stress; concerts; dramas; day-care centers; country dance lessons; sporting events; and small group opportunities, to name a few. Through these events and opportunities, people develop new relationships with other Christians. They gain exposure to the church and the gospel. Eventually they may feel comfortable enough to try out the worship service.

The following story has reached legendary proportions in church growth circles but it illustrates the point. John Wimber, while planting a new church, set out to discover the unique needs of his community. He and his team surveyed the area and found potty training to be the number one concern among area families. The findings puzzled them. They didn't know how to respond since potty training doesn't seem to be a highly spiritual value. So they turned to the Bible. They came across Proverbs 22:6, which reads: "Train up children in the way they should go. . . ." Supported by a biblical foundation they set up a potty training seminar. They hired a well-known local psychologist, promoted the event, and had a wonderful turn out. Each participant signed in (giving Wimber the ability to follow up on them later) and learned something of value. Many of the seminar participants eventually joined that new church start. That's a side-door approach to first base.

The best strategy uses both side-door and front-door opportunities. The more opportunities people have to meet believers, the more likely they'll come back. The more they hear the gospel, the more likely they'll commit their lives to it. Before they can get home, people have to get to first base. Mission-focused churches build bridges and offer events to help seekers get through the door. (For more first base ideas, see chapter 4).

- Second Base—Growth. No one wants to be stuck on first base. In baseball, we want to get home. But to get home, we need to move to second base. Second base represents growth. It includes opportunities for people of all faith levels to learn about Jesus.

Growth opportunities range from practical living seminars (marriage, parenting, midlife crisis, and so on), practical faith classes (understanding the Gospels, discovering Jesus, and so forth), to personal spirituality courses (how to develop a dynamic prayer life, prayer for healing, and so on).

When designing growth opportunities, it's important to keep the following in mind:

- We can't force people to grow. Negative appeals admonishing people to move ahead in the faith always backfire. Such appeals demotivate people. We can, however, entice people to try a class or seminar by creating events around their needs. By listening, we can discover the hunger in their lives and respond through appropriate classes.

The wind and the sun were holding a contest. They wanted to see which of them could make the man below take off his coat. The wind was the first to try. It blew as hard as it could. But the harder it blew, the tighter the man held on to his coat. Then the sun took its turn. It showered the man with warmth. The man eventually felt so comfortable that he decided to take off his coat.

As we continually hold up the gospel, God creates a desire for learning in people. When congregations offer relevant opportunities to grow, many people will respond. Through invitations from the pulpit and other forms of advertising, God draws people into maturity. Growth happens through invitation, not confrontation.

- People respond to people. One of the best ways to grow a church is to encourage members to invite their friends. One of the best ways to grow people is to have committed members bring their friends to appropriate growth opportunities.
- People want to know what's in it for them. Why should people give up some of their valuable, limited time to come to a class or seminar? What will they take home? Mission-driven congregations continually seek to answer that question as they market their growth opportunities.
- The most effective education programs today start with the needs of the customer. In a personalized economy, the customer rules.

That principle makes need-driven classes imperative. Need-driven classes, however, do not need to be non-biblical. People want to know how the Bible relates to real life. They want to apply the truths of the gospel to their daily walks. As they do, the gospel captures and transforms them. By listening to the Spirit and to the "customer," churches can keep their classes current and relevant.

- People will not all take the same path. Effective education programs offer people choices. Providing a plan or process for growth will be helpful for many (see below). A variety of growth opportunities, however, will reach a variety of people. (See appendix A for growth ideas.)
- Third Base—Ministry. Many congregations believe that the key to involvement is found in committees. They make the mistake of expecting the pastor to do the ministry while the members, through committees, manage the church. But it should be the other way around. The pastor should manage the congregation (with the help of a leadership board) and train the members to do the work of ministry. Certainly, God has equipped some members with the gifts of administration and management. They make excellent committee people. But other members have been gifted to pray for the sick, teach Sunday school, offer words of encouragement and hope, care for hurting people, do research for sermons, and so on. Mission-driven churches involve people by streamlining management systems and maximizing ministry opportunities.

A pastor tells about making a hospital call on the way to a church council meeting. As often happens, the pastor felt as inspired from the visit as did the patient. The church council meeting, on the other hand, turned out to be another night of tense, loud discussions. During the meeting the pastor thought to himself, "Why should I have all the fun ministering to people while the members sit in boring or even hostile meetings?" That night he made the decision to phase out all unnecessary committees and to train people to do the work of the ministry.

People grow in their faith as they give themselves away through service. When they put their talents into action they experience a sense of significance and purpose. Mission-driven churches take those principles seriously and train and equip individuals for ministry. They encourage their members to find a meaningful place to serve by helping them discover their God-given gifts.[6] They also develop opportunities that offer people a place where they can use those newly discovered gifts. Mission-driven congregations continually invite people to discover, develop, and use their gifts to serve God through the church.

- Home Plate—Missions. Where ministry (in terms of this strategy) focuses on serving within the church, missions focuses on serving outside of the church. Mission-driven congregations train their people to go out and help a dying world. They teach relationship building skills that empower their members to share their faith. They also provide opportunities for people to do missions locally, nationally, and internationally. (See appendix A for mission ideas.)

Community Church of Joy summarizes its strategy for the last three bases as follows: Every member is a minister and every minister has a mission. Again, discipleship is not so much a matter of membership but of involvement and participation. This strategy seeks to provide people with the necessary opportunities to keep them running around the bases. (Here the analogy deviates some from baseball.) Growing people make an on-going commitment to Jesus through worship, growth, ministry, and missions.

Strategy #2—A youth ministry. One youth ministry describes its strategy in terms of five G's:

1) Grace—God comes to us. This youth ministry creates opportunities to help it connect with young people. For example, the church sponsors outreach events at the church, Bible studies on the school campus, fifth quarters (fun events after football or basketball games), and so forth.
2) Growth—God changes us. Through Sunday school classes dealing with topics of interest to students, Bible studies, and seminars, the youth begin to grow in faith.
3) Groups—God nurtures us. Small groups provide the opportunity for fellowship, spiritual growth, and accountability. These groups offer an intimacy in relationships that classes and seminars cannot provide.

4) Gifts—God empowers us. This youth ministry commits itself to helping young people discover their God-given gifts and talents.

5) Giving—God uses us. Having discovered their gifts, the students give themselves away through missions and ministry. Opportunities for service include singing in a touring choir, working with the homeless, missions trips to other parts of the world, community service, and so on.

Strategy #3—Christ Lutheran Church, Southwick, Massachusetts. Christ Lutheran Church uses the following continuum to describe its strategy:

1) Prospect. By *prospect* the congregation means its target audience—unchurched Baby Boomers. The church has designed several substrategies to build bridges to its prospects, including doing occasional direct mailings and equipping members to invite their friends.

2) Friend. "Friends" are those who have shown a favorable interest in the congregation by attending worship or other activities. Again, several substrategies focus on assimilating these new friends. Ideas include a new friends class designed to introduce people to the church.

3) Member. Friends become members when they make a commitment to the church by officially joining it. Members are encouraged to get involved through a wide range of growth opportunities, from small groups to retreats to seminars.

4 and 5) Leader and Servant. Leaders and servants commit themselves to the beliefs and spiritual disciplines valued by the congregation. The congregation seeks to grow leaders and servants through special times of training.

Again, a well-designed strategy makes intentional the church's mission and keeps the church focused. A strategy gives the mission statement its legs by providing the plan for carrying out the mission.

One pastor puts it this way:

> . . . no strategy is a strategy. Having nothing planned is a plan that will hinder what the Spirit would desire in the life of a young Christian. . . . We also want to avoid the idea that just

having one program or method is going to be the fail-safe solution to the issue of disciplemaking. . . . That one program is effective in only a limited number of people's lives.

THE PROCESS

Once a congregation answers the question, "How will we carry out the mission?" (strategy), it gets even more specific by asking, "What path or paths will lead our people into discipleship? Once they're in the door, where do they go? How do they grow?" (process).

When it comes to growth, not all people will take the same path. Some will jump from one class to another with no apparent rhyme or reason. And yet, through that process they hear the gospel and grow in faith. Mission-driven churches create all kinds of programs and classes that enable that kind of growth.

On the other hand, many people desire a more systematic approach to their faith journey. They want to know where to start and where they're headed. Designing a clear process gives the church a tool to help guide people into growth. The process also offers those who want to grow a path to follow.

A few years ago some of us on staff at Community Church of Joy spent several hours reviewing our ministry. We reminded ourselves of our mission: leading the unchurched into responsible discipleship. We understood discipleship as a lifelong journey. We had the opportunities for growth in place. We felt good about our strategy. But we lacked a discernable pathway to maturity—a process for those who are more systematic in their approach to life and faith. We couldn't identify a clear road for people to follow.

Not long after that discussion, I heard Rick Warren, pastor of Saddleback Valley Community Church, in Mission, Viejo, California, speak about a program of seminars offered at his church. It was exactly what we needed. So we borrowed Rick's curriculum, adapted it to fit Lutheran theology, and turned it into the **Incredible Journey Seminars**. Other congregations use a similar approach.

INCREDIBLE JOURNEY SEMINARS

The **Incredible Journey Seminars** consist of three seminars, with each seminar lasting three hours. All three seminars are offered simultaneously once a month. Each seminar seeks to lead people into intimacy with God and help them grow in their faith. **The Incredible Journey Seminars** offer people a clear, easy-to-follow starting point for getting involved in growth and service at Joy.

Seminar #1—How to Know God Personally. The first three-hour seminar serves as both the beginning of **The Incredible Journey** and as the new member orientation. It includes small group opportunities and large group presentations. As the seminar begins, the large group breaks into small groups. People stay with the same group for all small group events during the seminar.

The agenda looks something like this:

Hour 1

- Welcome/introduction to the seminar
- Small group get-acquainted time using a nonthreatening ice-breaker (for example, ask everyone to describe their favorite room in the house when they were eight years old).
- A presentation by the senior pastor on the story of Community Church of Joy. He talks about the struggles and joys of growing a church from 87 worshippers to 3000. He uses the opportunity to share the vision and mission of Joy.
- 10-minute break (including refreshments)

Hour 2

- Small group discussion—"How I came to Community Church of Joy"
- An inspirational, practical presentation on how to develop a relationship with God. It includes a brief introduction to Martin Luther and focuses on the Lutheran understanding of the gospel. At the end of the presentation each person assesses his or her spiritual journey using the spiritual journey survey described in chapter 6.
- A 10-minute break (including refreshments)

Hour 3

- Small group discussion—another get-acquainted exercise
- A presentation on how the church can support people in their spiritual journey. This presentation includes an overview of growth opportunities. Suggestions are given on where people

might start in their growth journey based on their spiritual journey survey. Some time is also devoted to a discussion of how the church manages its financial resources.

- A question and answer time.
- The seminar ends as people fill out the appropriate forms for joining the church. Again, this first seminar enables the participants, should they so choose, to join the church. Some may choose not to join at that time. Instead they may decide to hang around awhile and get more involved before making the commitment to membership.

Seminar #2—How to Deepen Your Friendship with God. Once people have completed the first seminar they are encouraged and invited to move on to the second seminar. In this seminar participants discuss the habits of the Christian life: worship, prayer, devotions, Bible study, giving, and small group involvement. Practical guidance, resources, and ideas are given in each area. As with the first seminar, the event features several small group experiences. The seminar attenders receive a prayer journal to get them started on the road to daily devotions.

Seminar #3—How to Discover Your God-Given Potential. This seminar focuses on three main areas: our God-given personality, our God-given gifts, and service. Each individual has the opportunity to take a gift survey. Once the survey is completed, the person meets with a gift counselor who matches the individual's gifts to appropriate areas of service and ministry in the congregation.

Once people have been through all three seminars, they become a part of the leadership circle. These leaders meet regularly with the pastors to receive ministry updates and training, and to discuss together the mission of Joy.

Classes designed to help people grow further support each seminar. For instance, after the first seminar people can continue their growth through classes such as "Discover the Bible," or "Discover Jesus," opportunities that focus on the basics of the faith. After the second seminar, people can take prayer seminars, Bible book studies, and so on. These opportunities assume a deeper level of maturity than first level classes. Another level of classes follows the third seminar. This process offers a comfortable, easy-to-follow path for people trying to figure out where to begin or where to go next. The **Incredible Journey Seminars** serve as a springboard into a lifetime of growth and service.

Another process might involve the development of a training school that uses a format similar to that of a college or university. On this path people take certain required courses over a period of time. For example, in a one-year period they might be required to take four classes, each lasting five weeks. These classes introduce the beliefs and faith habits the congregation values. The curriculum draws from personal living courses (building relationships, dealing with stress, and so on) to classes on the Christian faith classes (Bible book studies, how to give away one's faith, and so on.) After completing each level (which can usually be done in one year) the participants receive a certificate. After completing the entire school in three to four years, participants can be honored at a special graduation ceremony.

Again, the process gives people a discernable pathway to growth. The more processes a church can offer, the more people it will be able to serve and nurture.

DREAMSHOP

1) Define your congregation's current strategy for reaching and nurturing people. (Every congregation has a strategy, even if it hasn't been defined. No strategy is a strategy.) Is the strategy working? Does it offer people a concise, concrete picture of the congregation's vision for continual growth?

2) If the congregation has no defined strategy, or one that isn't working, ask the following questions: What do we want to have happen in the lives of our members? How do we visualize the transition from seeker to participant? How can we actively encourage people to grow? Map out a strategy for growth.

3) What classes are currently being offered in your congregation? What faith level do they assume? New believer? Lifelong church goer? Seeker? Are there ample opportunities for those new in the faith to get started? If not, what kinds of classes might you offer for them? How do you find out what might interest them? Are you offering a wide variety of classes? If not, what classes,

seminars, or small group experiences do you need to offer in the
near future?

4) If a new person asked how to get started in his or her faith journey
at your church, what would you say? What process or processes
have been developed to guide people into growth? What process
or processes can be offered?

A well-designed strategy in combination with an effective process
makes intentional and gives direction to the church's mission of
connecting with secular people and leading them into discipleship.
Once a strategy is in place, mission-driven congregations then focus
on nurturing disciples. They begin by drawing a profile of a disciple.

THE DISCIPLE PROFILE

•

profile: a short, vivid biographical and character sketch;
a graph, diagram, writing, etc., presenting or summarizing
data relevant to a particular person or thing.

—NEW WORLD DICTIONARY

CHAPTER 6

THE PROFILE OF
A DISCIPLE

•

For this reason I bow my knees before
the Father, from whom every family in
heaven and on earth takes its name. I
pray that, according to the riches of his
glory, he may grant that you may be
strengthened in your inner being with
power through his Spirit, and that
Christ may dwell in your hearts through
faith, as you are being rooted and
grounded in love. I pray that you may
have the power to comprehend, with all
the saints, what is the breadth and
length and height and depth, and to
know the love of Christ that surpasses
knowledge, so that you may be filled
with all the fullness of God.

(EPHESIANS 3:14-19)

Follow me. Two simple words. Two words that have transformed millions of lives, yet words filled with staggering implications: "If any want to become my followers let them deny themselves and take up their cross" (Mark 8:34). "Whoever comes to me and does not hate father and mother, wife and children, brothers and sisters, yes, even life itself, cannot be my disciple. Whoever does not carry the cross and follow me cannot be my disciple" (Luke 14:26-27).

Such demands offend today's individualists and rub them the wrong way. These statements of Jesus go against everything free agents stand for. And yet as believers we know that following Jesus, being in relationship with God, will meet the deep need they have for meaning in life.

Mission-driven churches see their purpose as connecting with these unchurched free agents. By doing so, outreach-oriented congregations seek to provide opportunities in which the Spirit can move seekers into dynamic discipleship, lead the unchurched into responsible church membership, help people grow from infancy to maturity, and turn spectators into active participants. These congregations commit themselves to carrying out Paul's vision of the mission of the Church:

> . . . to equip the saints for the work of ministry, for building up the body of Christ, until all of us come to the unity of the faith and of the knowledge of the Son of God, **to maturity, to the measure of the full stature of Christ. We must no longer be children,** tossed to and fro and blown about by every wind of doctrine, by people's trickery, by their craftiness in deceitful scheming. But speaking the truth in love, **we must grow up in every way into him** who is the head, into Christ. . . . (Eph. 4:12-13).

So how do we motivate and lead a self-centered culture into the radical nature of discipleship? Once they're in the door, what do we want people to learn? What do we want them to value? The disciple profile helps address these issues.

THE DISCIPLE PROFILE

The mission statement answers the question, "What has God called us to do?" The strategy answers the question, "How will we carry out the mission?" The process answers the question, "What path will lead our people into growth once they're in the door?" And the disciple profile answers the question, "What do we want our people to learn and become?"

The disciple profile defines or pictures what a disciple—or believer—looks like for a particular congregation. It focuses on the vital signs or habits that keep a relationship, specifically a relationship with God, healthy. It also identifies the values and beliefs that the congregation wants to instill in its members.

DEFINING DISCIPLESHIP

To develop the disciple profile, congregations should begin by defining what they mean by *discipleship*. The following definition might be helpful:

1) Discipleship is a one-time event. Disciples are people who have been adopted into God's family of faith through Jesus Christ. They've been transformed by God's grace.

Zacchaeus was a tax collector. He worked for the enemy of his people—Rome. In addition to betraying his people, he robbed them. He overtaxed them and pocketed the profit. His people considered him a traitor, viewing him and others like him as despised sinners.

That all changed, however, when Zacchaeus met Jesus. As Jesus walked through Jericho, Zacchaeus climbed a tree to see him. Jesus noticed Zacchaeus and invited himself over to Zacchaeus' house. Though we have no idea what happened in that private meeting, we do know that Zacchaeus emerged a changed man. After spending time with Jesus, Zacchaeus pledged to give half of his possessions to the poor. And he offered to compensate fourfold those he had cheated. Jesus invited Zacchaeus into a relationship with himself— a relationship of grace that transformed Zacchaeus' life (Luke 19:1-10). And that relationship made Zacchaeus a disciple.

Karen had been a prostitute on the streets of Chicago since the age of 12. When she was 17 a caring police officer rescued her. He brought her to a camp filled with other hurting teenagers. My friend Tom happened to be one of the speakers at that camp. He spoke about God's unconditional love and about how God accepted each of those young people. After his message Karen approached him and said, "You're a liar. God doesn't love me. He can't. Christians don't love me. You don't accept people like me. You're lying."

Karen had caught Tom off guard. He tried to tell her again about God's love. She listened for awhile and said, "Prove it." So Tom turned to the biblical story of the woman caught in adultery. When he was done Karen asked, "Is it true? Can Jesus really forgive me? Can he really change me?" Moved by the grace of God, Karen surrendered her life, her past, and her hurts to Jesus.

Several years later a woman came up to Tom after one of his messages. She said, "You don't recognize me, do you?" Tom couldn't believe his eyes. It was Karen. She told him that she had just finished Bible school. She was about to enter a ministry working with young girls who had backgrounds similar to her own. God had absolutely transformed her life. He had set her free to be his disciple.

People become disciples at the moment of rebirth:

> Do you not know that all of us who have been baptized into Christ Jesus were baptized into his death? Therefore we have been buried with him by baptism into death, so that, just as Christ was raised from the dead by the glory of the Father, so we too might walk in newness of life. (Romans 6:3-4)

Disciples are people whose lives have been graced by God. To belong to God is to be Jesus' disciple. To be a believer in Jesus is to be his disciple. The distinction sometimes made between believers and disciples has no biblical warrant. They are one and the same. As a result, disciples come in many different shapes and sizes. Some are new to the faith. Others have been following Jesus for a life time. Some feel their relationship with God is stagnating. Others have become apathetic. Some are enjoying a growing intimacy with God. Some might be trying to make the faith of their parents their own. The point is, regardless of where people are in their faith journey, they are disciples of Jesus by virtue of God's grace. We become disciples when God makes us a part of his family.

2) However, discipleship means growth. One never really arrives but continually grows:

> As you therefore have received Christ Jesus as the Lord, continue to live your lives in him, rooted and built up in him and established in the faith, just as you were taught, abounding in thanksgiving. (Col. 2:6-7)

Jan and I have two children, Alycia and Michael. Since their births we have prayed that they would grow to be all God created them to be. Like every parent we want our children to mature into responsible, productive adults. And like every parent we look for and encourage certain signs of growth in that maturing process. When our children were little, we watched for motor skill development. We anticipated and enjoyed their growing use of language. As they entered school we monitored their intellectual and social development, looking for signs of wholeness and health. Our daughter's entry into her teens has provided some interesting new signs of maturity. We see the mood swings, the up-and-down relationships, and the stretch toward independence. As difficult as they sometimes are, we find comfort in the normalcy of such signs. Our son stands on the threshold of adolescence himself. We anticipate growing muscles, an interest in girls, and a voice change.

At each stage of life, our expectations for our children change. We can't expect a two-year-old to respond to life like a fourteen-year-old. (One should be more mature than the other, though sometimes I'm not sure which!) However, we can expect and encourage all children to continue growing no matter what their age. And as our children grow we attend to those things that lead to health and maturity. We feed, love, clothe, house, teach, and discipline them. Without that kind of care our children might not grow into mature adults. Failing to focus on their welfare might rob them of their potential.

The same can be said about disciples. Discipleship is a process of growth. People move from infancy in their faith to maturity. Throughout the process we can look for certain vital signs of health and vitality. We can nourish and support each other along the way. Each disciple has his or her own relationship with God, and the character and maturity of that relationship will depend in part on how long the person has been following Christ. But we can encourage all disciples to keep growing.

3) Discipleship centers on a relationship with God. Relationships are dynamic. They grow as people spend time together getting to know each other. They stagnate and even die if people ignore each other or take the relationship for granted.

When Jan and I were married in 1979, we didn't start out by writing a list of rules we would follow to keep the relationship strong. Instead, our love for each other, our relationship, shapes and motivates our behavior. As is true of any relationship, however, we've discovered certain habits that keep our marriage fresh and alive. We make time for weekly date nights, daily times of conversation, listening, meaningful touch, prayer, and romance. While these habits naturally flow out of our love for each other, they also require intentionality. Making them a priority helps keep our marriage healthy. They also mature our love for each other by helping us get to know each other better.

Discipleship is a relationship with God. It centers on following Jesus Christ. Disciples are people who've said "yes" to God's "yes," answering the call to follow Jesus. They live in response to God's grace, finding motivation for life in God's love and forgiveness. They seek to live their lives with a whole new mindset—from the perspective of children of God, rather than from the perspective of a secular culture. Disciples don't follow rules to keep their relationship with God strong. God's love for them and their love for God keep the relationship fresh. But as with any relationship, disciples develop certain habits that help them be intentional about their walk with Christ (for example, worship, prayer, and so forth). Mission-driven congregations offer guidance for believers on how to grow in their relationship with God. They encourage people to spend time getting to know God and experiencing God's love for them.

Following Jesus as his disciple is a lifelong process. It includes participating in his body, experienced through the local congregation. When we learn about God and God's work, develop relationships with other Christians, and take advantage of opportunities to carry out God's ministry and mission, the Spirit deepens our relationship with God. The Spirit gently leads us back to the cross each day, reminding us that we love, because God first loved us (1 John 4:19).

Undergirded by a solid understanding of discipleship, mission-driven churches then create a disciple profile. To use business terminology, they determine what the end product looks like—what they want people to learn, value, and become. They then design programs to help people move toward that goal.

An Example

For the last several years a mission-driven congregation has been focusing on what it means to make disciples. They've struggled with how to measure the effectiveness of that mission. They wanted to give clearer direction to their ministry of reaching the irreligious and leading them into a growing faith. So they have created a disciple profile by identifying several vital signs of a growing Christian. This church believes that, just as certain vital signs indicate the health of an individual or relationship, so other vital signs can indicate the spiritual health of a person or a church.

The following offers an overview of one congregation's disciple profile, their understanding of the vital signs of a growing Christian. Notice how this disciple profile focuses on the "faith habits" that keep a relationship vibrant. A disciple:

1) Worships regularly. The Bible encourages us to meet together as believers (Heb. 10:24-25). Many seekers begin their discipleship journey by worshipping once or twice a month. As the gospel continues to shape their lives, their hunger for worship grows. This congregation encourages a growing commitment to regular, consistent worship attendance.

2) Takes time for personal devotions. Jesus made prayer a high priority. He invites his followers to do the same. Developing intimacy with God through prayer and devotions keeps people refreshed. It also keeps them motivated on their discipleship journey.

3) Is committed to growing in her or his knowledge of the faith. Disciples commit themselves to grow in their relationship with God. That means participating in at least one growth opportunity outside of worship. That involvement might include joining a small group, attending midweek worship, enrolling in a prayer seminar, or taking an adult education course. The more people grow, the more they want to grow.

4) Gives cheerfully of his or her financial resources. Having received God's best gift through Jesus Christ, disciples respond by giving

of themselves through their financial resources. The Bible continually encourages believers to give generously (Mal. 3:8-10; Luke 6:38; 1 Cor. 8-9). For most new believers, giving money runs contrary to their values. They've been raised in a hoard-it-for-myself culture. Besides, they reason that the church was doing fine financially before they came. The buildings were up before they started coming. The staff was being paid before they joined the congregation. The church apparently doesn't need their money. But as the love of God permeates their lives (and pocketbooks), he sets them free to be cheerful givers. Many churches lift up tithing as a goal.

5) Is involved in missions. Disciples also grow in giving their time. As people pour themselves into others, they discover that they actually receive more than they give. Disciples commit themselves to reaching out to others by sharing their faith through words and actions.

With that profile in mind, the congregation then creates classes and programs to help people develop those faith habits. Other profiles might include the faith or values statements to which the congregation adheres. For example, a congregation might define a disciple as one who believes in the triune God, has been baptized, upholds the authority of Scripture, receives the sacraments regularly, seeks to shape life around the values of the gospel, upholds the dignity of all people, can articulate his or her faith story, embraces the Lutheran Confessions, and so forth.

A congregation might also identify expected levels of involvement. For example, Lyle Schaller, among others, lists the following characteristics of an incorporated member. A disciple:

1) Can list at least seven new friends made in church.
2) Can identify his/her spiritual gifts.
3) Is involved in at least one role/task/ministry appropriate to his or her spiritual gifts.
4) Is involved in a small group or on-going adult education opportunities.
5) Demonstrates a regular financial commitment to the church.
6) Personally identifies with the goals of the congregation.
7) Exhibits a regular worship commitment to the church.

8) Is excited about identifying unchurched friends and family members, inviting them to church, and helping them get involved.

BENEFITS OF A DISCIPLE PROFILE

Creating a disciple profile offers a church at least two benefits:

1) A disciple profile helps facilitate a climate in which people can grow. A disciple profile helps make intentional the mission of the church and then keeps the congregation focused on its purpose: helping people grow in their relationship with Christ. Along with the strategy and process, it sets the agenda for the kind of teaching and nurturing opportunities the church wants to offer (see appendix A).

Certainly a disciple profile can degenerate into law, elitism, and judgmentalism if not rooted firmly in grace. Only God knows the heart of a person. God through the Holy Spirit initiates, establishes, and nurtures a relationship with each disciple. The lack of such a profile, on the other hand, can result in an unfocused mission and disciples who do not grow.

2) A disciple profile enables a congregation to measure its effectiveness. Congregations committed to helping people grow must find a way to determine whether or not it's happening. For example, when I decided to lose 30 pounds, I began a process of changing my life. I discovered that successful diets require a whole new way of living, thinking, eating, and exercising. Healthy diets move people from one way of viewing life and food to another. In order to measure the effectiveness of that new life change I set a goal. I determined how much weight I wanted to lose and then every day I measured my progress by stepping on a scale. Ultimately, (for the most part) if the dieter never loses weight, the dieter has not really changed. Or the diet hasn't worked. (I did lose the weight!)

One way to measure a congregation's effectiveness is to use a spiritual journey survey. This survey enables members to assess their own spiritual growth. By answering a series of questions they can plot where they are in their faith journey. The survey might look like this:[1]

1) This first assessment question focuses on your view of your faith. (You may check as many items as you think apply to you.)

At this point in my faith journey I am:

_____ Unsure of what I believe

_____ Curious

_____ Investigating Christianity

_____ Trying to make my parents' faith my own

_____ Wrestling with doubts

_____ New to the faith

_____ A believer in Christ

_____ Deepening my commitment to Christ

_____ Becoming an active follower of Christ

_____ Moving into service and ministry

2) The second question focuses on your actual growth journey.

At this point in my faith journey I am:

_____ Floundering

_____ Going backwards

_____ Stagnating

_____ Craving something more

_____ Interested in growing but unsure how to begin

_____ Needing help to ask the right questions

_____ Starting to grow

_____ Actively learning about my faith

_____ Interested in serving

_____ Actively serving

3) The third question focuses on your relationship to the congregation.

At this point in my spiritual journey I:

_____ Feel like a stranger

_____ Feel like a welcomed newcomer

_____ Need help making new friends

_____ Am making new friends in the church

_____ Have developed several friends in the church

_____ Enjoy several close relationships with people in the church

Two additional questions might be included: How can the church better serve you as you continue your faith journey? What seminars or classes would you find helpful?

This survey can be filled out anonymously. The members keep one copy for themselves. They turn in another one, just like it, to the church. The staff can then use the results to gain a better understanding of their people and design appropriate growth opportunities.

It might also be helpful to encourage people to set faith journey goals. This form, too, can be very simple:

As I continue my faith journey I want to set the following goals to help me grow: (for example, I will worship two times per month; I will commit to taking one Bible study class this fall; I will set aside five minutes per day for devotions and prayer; and so on.)

Again, people can keep one copy of the goals for themselves. The other copy, filled out anonymously, goes to the staff for further ministry evaluation. Each year those goals can be evaluated and updated.

In addition to a spiritual journey survey, tracking the numerical growth in certain ministry areas offers another way to measure ministry effectiveness. Almost every congregation, for example, measures the financial giving of its members. This measurement enables the congregation to put together a realistic budget. It also raises red flags should giving start to decrease.

Tracking membership also enables congregations to measure the health of the organization. If the statistics show a decline in membership, the congregation can start asking "why" with the hope of reversing the trend. Maybe the problem is a big back door, or a recession causing many to move out of the area, or the fallout from a controversial decision, and so on. If the statistics show a growth in membership, the congregation can find out why and build on what they learn.

Worship attendance can provide great insights into the well-being of the church. More often than not, worship attendance tells the real story, for worship attendance, not membership, demonstrates involvement. Is worship attendance down? Why? Is it up? Why?

If involvement in small groups or adult education classes fails to grow, the congregation can investigate by again asking "why?" Maybe people choose not to attend because the classes don't speak to the needs or issues they care about. Perhaps the classes are scheduled at a bad time. Maybe a foundation of growth hasn't been properly laid, and so on.

DREAMSHOP

1) What values and beliefs does your congregation want to teach? What does it mean to be involved in your congregation? What does a disciple look like?
2) Based on the answers to those questions, develop a disciple profile.
3) Create a tool that enables your members to periodically evaluate their faith journey.
4) Create a tool that enables your members to periodically set new growth goals.

Mission-driven congregations seek to provide relevant opportunities for people to discover the good news of grace—that God loves us. Mission-driven congregations encourage involvement and growth, so that the Spirit might nurture people and daily draw them to God.

Driven by their commitment to create a climate for growth, mission-driven congregations continually wrestle with the following questions: Are we addressing seekers in a way that enables them to hear Christ's invitation to discipleship? Are we providing doors to involvement that help people mature in their faith? Are people being rooted and built up in the faith? Are they growing in their knowledge and experience of God? Are they growing in intimacy with God? Are we helping them move from spectators to participants in the faith and in the life of the church? Are we effectively making disciples?

But perhaps their most challenging question is: How do we transform our congregation into a mission? How do we go about implementing change?[1]

CHANGE

•

change: to make different; alter; modify;
to cause to pass from one form, composition, or state to
another;
to transform.

—MERIT STUDENTS DICTIONARY

CHAPTER 7

TRANSFORMING A CONGREGATION INTO A MISSION

•

For surely I know the plans I have for
you, says the LORD, plans for your
welfare and not for harm, to give you a
future with hope.

(JEREMIAH 29:11)

When trains were first invented, several experts expressed caution. They feared that if a train moved at the frightful speed of fifteen miles per hour, passengers would suffer nosebleeds. They also predicted that passengers would suffocate when going through tunnels.

In 1881 the New York YMCA announced typing lessons for women. Some protested on the grounds that the female constitution would break under the strain.

Joseph Coppersmith was arrested for trying to sell stock in a company formed to sell a new product—the telephone. Experts declared that all well-informed people knew it was impossible to transmit the human voice over a wire.

Change never comes easily, for change, more often than not, takes us out of our comfort zone. As a result, in the face of change, people tend to withdraw and do business as usual. For example, some people seek to do ministry in the 1990s and beyond with a 1950s mindset. They believe that they can be more effective if they simply do what they've always done—but do more of it and do it better. In other words, they believe that doing the same thing harder will produce new results. So they cling to the past in a changing, uncertain world.

One thing, however, is certain: In our post-Christendom Era, many of the old ways of doing things no longer work. As Robert Schuller often says, to be effective today the congregation must die as a church and be reborn as a mission. That means change.

THE NATURE OF CHANGE

Change is the process of moving from one thing to another: from an old skill to a new skill, an old era to a new era, an old mission to a new mission, old wineskins to new wineskins, old methods to new methods, from the old form to the new form, and so on. Change moves us from the past to the future. But through the process of change we usually go through a period of conflict and chaos. We move from certainty to uncertainty, from stability to insecurity. We experience the death of the old and suffer through all of the struggle, doubt, and hurt that goes with grief. Once we've been through the death of the old, however, we begin to experience the resurrection of the new. Grief turns to joy, struggle grows into satisfaction, doubt becomes faith, and hurt is healed.

FOUR STAGES OF CHANGE

Drs. Cynthia Scott and Dennis Jaffe tell us that when making a commitment to transform a church into a mission, the congregation can expect to go through four stages of change: denial, resistance, exploration, and commitment.[1]

Stage 1—Denial. In the face of change, people tend to focus on the past and deny the reality of the present, for change places us into the hands of uncertainty and even fear.

While in college I discovered something about elephants that has much to say about our response to change. I learned that when training an elephant, the trainer chains one leg of the animal to a tree. For a while, the elephant tugs at the chain, trying to loose itself. Eventually, however, the elephant becomes conditioned to believe that it cannot escape. After a period of time the elephant's chain is shackled to a stake in the ground. With one quick tug, the elephant could easily free itself. But whenever it feels the pull of the chain it remembers that it cannot move. The experiences of the past keep it chained to the stake. Instead of freeing itself, the elephant remains bound.

Congregations often find themselves bound by earlier conditioning as well. "We've always done it that way" keeps people chained to the past. Tradition can become an anchor holding congregations back rather than a rudder guiding them into the future. The past can limit their effectiveness for tomorrow. In fact, it can cause some to deny the reality of tomorrow and the need for change.

Though an elephant stays bound to the stake due to past conditioning, it can be freed. If a fire breaks out in the tent the elephant quickly forgets the past and changes. It immediately pulls the stake out of the ground and runs to freedom.

In our post-Christendom Era, the task of church leaders is to help congregations discover a new vision for the future. This might mean lighting a fire under the church (without burning down the ministry). It might mean discovering ways to make the congregation uncomfortable enough with its current work of maintenance that it wants to change.

Several factors can help move people out of denial and motivate a desire to change:

1) Seeing the need. Back in March 1962 *Newsweek* featured a story on 11-year-old Jerry Davis. The article was written while Jerry was in the hospital being treated for serious burns. He had been burned when he twice ran into his fire-engulfed house to save his two brothers. When reporters asked him if he felt afraid as he ran into the house he replied, "Yes, I was awfully afraid."

"Then how were you able to do it?" they asked.

"Well, I didn't want to lose my littlest brother just because I was 'ascared," Jerry answered.

Often times, when confronted with a pressing need, people will lay aside their fear of the unknown and change. Perhaps the need is the fact that 70% of the people living around a particular congregation are unchurched. Maybe it's a changing community. A once all-Anglo congregation finds itself in the middle of a Hispanic neighborhood. Whatever the need, it begins to motivate change.

2) Hurt. When people hurt enough, they will often risk change. For congregations, that hurt might be a decline in membership. Maybe the congregation finds itself struggling to pay the bills for the first time in recent memory. Perhaps individual members see their children leaving their denomination for other congregations or leaving the church all together.

One Sunday a pastor, who wanted to motivate change in his church, asked his members to look around. All they could see were people over the age of 50. He said to them, "This congregation is one generation away from extinction. We have to change to reach new generations." When people see their church hurting, they begin to ask what they can do to fix it and heal it.

While walking down the road one day a turtle fell into a large pothole. Try as it might, it couldn't climb out. Soon a rabbit friend hopped by. The rabbit tried to free the turtle, but the turtle remained stuck. "It's no use. I'll never get out of here," said the turtle. Friend after friend offered assistance, but the turtle was really stuck. "It's hopeless!" concluded the turtle.

Suddenly the turtle heard a noise. The noise grew louder and louder. The turtle poked up its head and spotted a tractor headed right toward him. Without another thought it stretched its legs and jumped out of the pothole to safety. His friends gathered around him and asked how he had freed himself. "We thought you couldn't get out!" they exclaimed. To which the turtle replied, "I couldn't. But then I saw a farmer approaching on a tractor, and I had to get out."

When congregations hurt enough, they often choose to change.

3) Information. To bring about change, leaders must constantly hold up a vision of the future. The more information they can provide, the more people will buy into the change. Sermons and forums on the changing culture, reaching irreligious people, and the mission of the church plant a new vision in the minds and hearts of the members. Information gives them a basis for evaluating change.

4) Hope. Change always means chaos. As people anticipate that chaos, they want to know what they'll gain from it. Is the disruption worth the end result? How will the change benefit me?

Will it really make a difference? By meeting the needs behind those questions (that is, the need for security and stability, the desire to make a difference, and so forth), leaders will find their people more eager to consider change.

Stage 2—Resistance. In this stage people move from denial to outright anger. Anxiety, depression, and even accusation mark the resistance period in the change process. People worry about how and where they will fit in the new form—what their place will be when the changes take hold. Several fear factors lead to resistance:

1) Fear of failure. As people face a proposed change, many fear that it might not work. Since they're entering into new territory, they often have no foundation on which to build. They feel like they're hanging out on a limb. Keeping things as they have always been brings comfort and stability. Change can lead to uncertainty, which can lead to fear of failure. And a fear of failure can paralyze people into inaction.

2) Fear of loss. Change often brings about loss. Losing something of value makes it difficult to change. In part, by losing something of value, people themselves feel devalued. In addition to that, if the loss does not seem worth the result, people will fight the proposed change. If the loss outweighs the gain, they'll resist the change. When moved out of their comfort zone, people become resistant.

3) Fear of losing identity. Because change means loss, it can also mean that things won't be the same again. Change always disrupts things. For example, adding a service can disrupt friendships as people choose to attend different services. Building a larger sanctuary can disrupt the small family feeling people once shared. Reaching out to the neighborhood can mean a bigger congregation and thus less intimacy. And with each change comes a change in identity. Things simply aren't like they used to be.

4) Fear of change in general. Some people naturally resist change, no matter how important the change might be.

Dealing with all of the emotions this stage produces is crucial. It's a tough stage to move through. But there are a number of strategies for overcoming resistance:

1) Celebrate the past. Give thanks for the wonderful work God did in the past through the congregation. Hold up the changed lives,

the sense of togetherness, and the important mission that took place. Remember the changes made in years past that kept the ministry alive and vibrant. Devaluing the past in order to move to the future simply devalues people. They will feel hurt at the suggestion that all their years of ministry were meaningless. Take time to remember, celebrate, and enjoy the past.

2) Let people process. When people initially resist change, the leaders tend to take it personally. But the leaders have thought about, prayed about, and planned the change for months. They've lived with the vision and have been completely captured by it. Usually the members haven't had the same opportunity to process the change. So, when a change is first proposed, people begin to ask their leaders the questions that change normally inspires. When that happens, leaders often assume the members do not trust them. They feel their leadership is being questioned. That, however, is not usually the case.

The members, like the leaders, need to think about and get comfortable with the new vision. They, too, need to pray through the change. Giving them the chance to do so will win their confidence. Use sermons, forums, and question and answer times to enable people to wrestle with the change. And allow them to express all of their emotions, even their negativity, to speed up the healing and acceptance process.

3) Acknowledge the chaos. As already stated, change produces chaos. Identify what the chaos might look like when the change takes place, and talk it through to make the chaos less threatening and more manageable.

4) Point to a new tomorrow. As people deal with the loss of the old, continually hold out the hope of the new. Focus on the resurrection—the new possibilities and the new mission—that will take place as a result of the proposed changes.

Stage 3—Explore. At this point, the focus slowly moves to the future. People begin to explore the possibilities of the new tomorrow. However, uncertainty continues to permeate the climate. People still feel unsure as to how to respond to the chaos and confusion. This stage can often lack focus. People continue to wonder what the change means for them personally. They wonder what they will have to give up.

Hold up the vision repeatedly to help people move through this stage. Set goals to enable them to see the light at the end of the tunnel. The new vision will begin to become tangible.

Stage 4—Expect commitment. In this stage the future drives the ministry. The focus becomes clearer and people begin to cooperate. They commit themselves to the new vision. As the church moves into the future, describing that future again and again remains essential. It's easy to fall into old habits. (Lyle Schaller says that people forget the vision in seven days.) Set and share long-term goals to keep people focused. And hold up the good news that will result from the change to keep people excited and energized. Though not easy, if congregations stick to it, their ministries can be transformed into missions.

KEYS FOR IMPLEMENTING CHANGE

Several key strategies for implementing change will help keep the momentum going:

1) Define and/or write the mission statement. In order for a church to be effective, it needs to know who it is and what its purpose is. A mission statement answers those questions. Write a mission statement to lay the foundation for change. Writing the statement keeps the focus on the mission. It also assumes the necessity for change to keep the mission on track. (See chapters 2 and 3 for more on developing a mission statement.)
2) Pray. Nothing great happens without prayer. Prayer empowers change. It gives birth to new visions. As people gather together in prayer around the vision, it unites and energizes them. Pray for the new vision in corporate settings to continually remind people of the importance of the change.

When Walt Kallestad first arrived at Community Church of Joy, God placed a vision for mission on his heart. That vision immediately met resistance. In his prayer time Walt sincerely asked God to either revive or remove those resistant to change. Within months, most of the anti-change group left. They either moved out of state or transferred to other churches.

Not everyone will buy into the change. Some people simply feel more comfortable in ministries they've enjoyed for years. That's all right. Though it's painful to lose them, perhaps these people will feel more significant and useful in another congregation. If God has truly birthed a new vision in the hearts of the leaders and members, giving permission for some to move on to another church will enable everyone to win.

3) Create an attitude of trust. Leaders must continually let their people know how much they care for them. Publish articles in your church newsletter, conduct forums, generally ensure access to any and all information, and maintain an open attitude to keep the climate of trust alive.

4) Focus on the mission, not the institution. Institutions resist change. Mission inspires it. Institutions look to the past. Mission looks to the future. Institutions are static. Mission is dynamic. Institutions focus on tradition. Mission focuses on people.

Community Church of Joy is in the process of relocating to a new site. Needless to say, it is a major change. Leaving the old campus is hard. Together we've built that place. Our children were baptized there. Many of us discovered a living, dynamic relationship with Jesus in that place. Marriages were strengthened, friendships were made, and families were put back together. The church property holds a lot of meaning and value for us. Leaving it will be difficult. However, focusing on the institution and the past would keep us chained to where we are. It would ultimately have a negative impact on our mission.

In order to help people adjust to the move, we continually focus on mission. In occasional messages and presentations we talk about the greater mission we will be able to carry out on the new campus. Highlighting the mission drives us to the future, even though leaving the past will be tough.

5) Begin with a small change to build momentum, trust, and success. Beginning with a major change in a congregation alien to change could prove disastrous. People need a chance to try on change, feel it, experience it, and see it work. Introduce a few small changes first to help people become comfortable with the concept

of change. As people see the positive impact those changes have, they'll be more willing to move ahead on bigger ones. Also, break down a major change into manageable parts to help ease some of the chaos.

6) Build ownership. Every congregation consists of different groups of people. Each group must buy into the vision. It is especially important that those who will ultimately implement the vision—whether staff members or lay leaders—have a sense of ownership. Bringing those people on board and valuing their input will help them accept the vision.

Identify the power brokers and invite their participation as soon as possible will also help build ownership. These power brokers might be the informal or formal leaders of the church. Take them out for lunch, pick their brains for ideas, include them in vision studies, and utilize their gifts. This will help them see that they're a vital part of the team.

Certainly the members who will vote for and finance the mission need to be won over. Through messages, prayer times, newsletters, and forums, they will begin to see and own the vision. Encourage them to visit churches that have already implemented similar changes to help them visualize the positives of the proposed change. Use the potential congregation exercise mentioned in chapter three to help them understand the need for change.

Ultimately, the best way to bring about change is to cultivate relationships with those most open to it. Once they've been reached, attention can be turned to those who seem resistant. Change happens by outgrowing the resistance.

7) Bring leaders to visioning conferences. Sometimes experts from outside the congregation can create a hunger for change that congregational leaders cannot. Getting away for a few days to dream under the direction of an innovative church can light the fire necessary for change. Or bring a change-oriented speaker into the church for a mini-conference to create a change-climate. Studying books on vision and mission can also be helpful.

8) Value your members. As said before, it's important not to value change by devaluing the past. The best policy, when at all possible, is to add something new, not to take something away. For example,

dropping a traditional service in favor of a new, contemporary service is a big mistake. It unnecessarily hurts and angers those who value traditional worship. Adding a contemporary service to the worship menu values both the traditionalists and those looking for new expressions of the faith.

9) Stick to it. Change takes tenacity. It can be derailed at any moment. The faint of heart need not apply. Leading change can be a very lonely, painful experience from time to time. Don't forget to put on your asbestos underwear.

10) Celebrate the change. As the new change begins to bear fruit, announce it, enjoy it, and celebrate it. Good news motivates more change.

11) Do it. There are a million reasons why it's easier not to change. But if God has placed in you a burning desire to transform your congregation into a mission, then do it. Don't let the process slow you down. Don't let lethargic, hesitant nay-sayers discourage you. With God's grace move ahead into tomorrow. For God is already in tomorrow preparing the best for your congregation.

DREAMSHOP

1) What two or three areas of ministry in your congregation need change? Why?

2) What resistance might be encountered if these ministries are changed?

3) How might these obstacles to change be overcome?

4) Who are the power brokers and leaders in the congregation?

5) What steps can be taken to win them over?

6) What steps can be taken to implement change within the congregation?

7) Choose one area in need of change. Map out a strategy for making it happen. Remember, this is a team process.

POSTSCRIPT

•

For while we were still weak, at the
right time Christ died for the ungodly.
Indeed, rarely will anyone die for a
righteous person—though perhaps for a
good person someone might actually
dare to die. But God proves his love for
us in that while we still were sinners
Christ died for us.

(ROMANS 5:6-8)

One day, while standing on a bridge, Winnie the Pooh noticed Eeyore floating below on the river. Pooh yelled down, "Did you fall into the river, Eeyore?"

"Yes, silly of me wasn't it?" replied Eeyore.

"Is the water cold today?" asked Pooh.

"Yes, the dampness, you know," said Eeyore.

"You really out to be more careful!" warned Pooh.

"Thanks," responded Eeyore.

After a moment of silence Eeyore asked, "Pooh, if it wouldn't be too much bother, would you mind rescuing me?"[1]

All around our churches live people who long to be rescued—rescued from meaninglessness, brokenness, emptiness, low self-esteem, and so on. They're waiting for someone who will love them enough to share a word of hope and encouragement with them. They're looking for a church that will believe in them enough to reach out to them—a congregation willing to take whatever risks necessary to lead them into a relationship with God through Christ.

Mission-driven churches seek to be in the business of connecting with those who feel like they're drowning. They continually find innovative ways to share the gospel so that secular people might know the transforming love of God. They commit themselves to doing whatever it takes to reach a lost and broken world.

God invites you and your church to that kind of ministry. Enjoy the journey!

> All authority in heaven and on earth has been given to me. Go therefore and make disciples of all nations, baptizing them in the name of the Father and of the Son and of the Holy Spirit, and teaching them to obey everything that I have commanded you. And remember, **I am with you always, to the end of the age.**
>
> —Jesus (Matt. 28:19-20)

APPENDIX A

Growth Ideas

•

The following letter was written to the editor of a Christian magazine:

> Dear Editor,
> It is difficult to attend Bible studies where everyone knows Scripture by heart and I'm just trying to figure out whether we are in the Old or New Testament. I feel that Jesus is urging me to study His word and I want to, but I don't know where to start. As the new list of Bible study classes at our church is posted, I keep hoping I'll see something like "Bible Study for Beginners—No Experience Necessary."[1]

After several years at Community Church of Joy, Ginny found herself on the church council. One night, at the end of a council meeting, several of us hung around for an informal discussion. We talked about the lack of participation by our people in Bible studies. Ginny offered her opinion. Having been a seeker, she could speak from personal experience. She said the problem wasn't necessarily a lack of hunger on the part of our people. Instead, she felt the problem was intimidation. People were intimidated by or afraid of Bible studies because they didn't know how to use their Bibles. Ginny had been there. She didn't know where to find certain books and was afraid she might be embarrassed in class. So, for awhile, she stayed away.

After listening to Ginny's story, we commissioned her right on the spot to develop a class for people totally unfamiliar with the Bible. The result was one of our most popular classes: Discover the Bible. This five-week course, in a fun, nonthreatening way, teaches people how to use the Bible. The class emphasizes making the Bible user friendly. Its purpose is to take away the fear of using the Bible, to give people the courage and confidence to attend Bible study classes. Congregations need that kind of innovative thinking if they want to transform seekers into disciples.

Listed below are several class, seminar, and small group ideas designed to encourage growth and participation. Each opportunity somehow contributes to the process of bringing people in, building them up, and sending them out. The majority of the ideas were developed by congregations. The Holy Spirit is still in the business of creating. Perhaps these suggestions will stimulate your creative juices and inspire you to develop similar classes and growth opportunities in your church. Denominational publishing houses and Christian bookstores might provide other helpful materials.

Doors to Involvement: Getting Them In

The following side-door events serve at least two purposes: 1) to attract people to the church, and 2) to help them build relationships with members of the church.

Country dance. Country music and dance is sweeping the nation. Offer a how-to class on country dance—The Shuffle, Two Step, or Line Dancing. This can be a great way to attract new people. At one church almost 80% of those registered for the country dance class were new to the congregation. During the class many of them made new friends. They had walked (or danced) onto the church campus and lived to tell about it, and eventually many of them felt drawn to experience the worship service.

Couple's hayride and barbecue is another great, nonthreatening opportunity to which members can invite their unchurched friends.

Bridge club. One church member had a friend with no church background. She knew her friend loved to play bridge, so she invited her to join the congregation's bridge club. After several weeks her friend became friends with the others in the club, and soon the friend started attending the worship services. Now she volunteers in the church passing out food and clothing for those in need.

Sporting activities. From family volleyball tournaments to softball leagues to competitive three-on-three basketball, sporting events offer great relationship-building opportunities. This strategy is most effective when teams commit to having at least some unchurched friends on it. Aerobic classes also provide not only a great workout but times to develop relationships, as well.

Craft classes. Classes on painting T-shirts, learning calligraphy, and sewing, like sports, can also attract people to the church.

Need-oriented seminars. Seminars targeted to specific need areas offer a non-threatening way for newcomers to get acquainted with a congregation. Seminars on marriage, divorce recovery, raising children, understanding youth, CPR, time management, and so on appeal to believers and nonbelievers. They provide a nice door into the church. They can also lead people to begin thinking about the Christian faith. As people see that the Bible speaks to everyday concerns, they find themselves wanting to know more.

Concerts. Concerts serve a role similar to that of seminars. A highly professional concert will lead many first-time guests to take a closer look at other aspects of the church.

Support groups. Sponsoring recovery and support groups lets the community know that the church cares. Many people have too much guilt or shame to enter a worship service. But out of their hurt they might try a Twelve Step group. Once they feel safe, they might make their way into the life of the congregation. Alcoholics Anonymous, Surviving Codependency, Divorce Recovery, Parents of Murdered Children, Grief and Loss Support, Parents Anonymous, Overeaters Anonymous, and a host of other recovery groups give people a touch point with the church—and with the God who can heal them.

Doors to Involvement: Entry Level Classes and Seminars

These classes target those new to the faith. Many of them also serve as outreach events.

Discover the Bible. A fun, easy-to-follow introduction to the Bible. The class focuses on how to make the Bible user friendly. It discusses the differences between the various versions, tips for finding the books in the Bible, and how to use the Bible in one's daily devotions. Through this class people gain the confidence and skills they need to move into Bible studies.

Discover Jesus. An intimate look at Jesus—who he is, what he did, and how he can affect our lives today.

Seekers and Doubters. A question-and-answer class open to anyone and everyone. During the first class, people have the opportunity to write down any questions they have about Christianity. Throughout the remaining sessions, each question is answered and discussed by the pastor or a well-trained lay person. This kind of class lets doubters know they're welcome—and not alone.

Discover the Exciting World of Prayer. An introduction to prayer. Other classes along this line might include, **Devotional Prayer** (developing a consistent devotional life) and **Praying With Your Children** (ideas on how to develop a devotional life for the entire family).

Understanding Yourself and Others. A fun-filled look at the personality God has created within us. In this class people begin to understand how God has wired them, their friends, and their family members. They also learn skills for building healthier relationships.

Living Anxiety Free. One out of nine people suffers from anxiety. One year I offered a four-part series of messages on the topic during worship. We followed it up with a class lead by a Christian counselor. We then followed that up with a small group experience. Many topics lend themselves well to such a progression, including marriage, parenting, depression, midlife crisis, anger, guilt, and so on.

Faith and Finances. Entry-level classes focus on the joy that comes when we invest in something greater than ourselves. Teaching stewardship is never easy, and teaching it to newcomers adds to the challenge. Most believers want to give, but many of them honestly don't know how. Their budgets seemingly can't handle it. Classes teaching people how to budget their money not only offer them a service but in the process show them how to give.

The Marriage Go-round. Asking well known-couples from the church to lead this class adds to its charm. Each week a different couple shares their experiences on a particular theme. For instance, the pastor and his or her spouse might focus on communication. The church president and her or his spouse might talk about romance. The adult education coordinator and his or her spouse might discuss prayer. People enjoy getting up close and personal with these church "celebrities." And personal stories have a powerful impact. Other marriage classes such as, Building a Strong Marriage, Keeping the Love Alive, and the like can combine personal stories, lecture, and Bible study.

Basic Christianity. A look at the essentials of the faith: grace, faith, forgiveness, prayer, the humanity and divinity of Jesus, and so on.

Raising Kids Alone. Hope for single parents in the form of helpful ideas, Bible study, and support.

Understanding Your Teenager. Insights into the unique values and attitudes of teenagers. Helpful suggestions on how to survive and thrive in a relationship with teens.

Bible Overview. A fast-paced, sweeping look at the Bible. How it was written, important characters, and essential stories.

Waist Watchers. This event can serve as both a support group and a class as people work together to discover ways to attain greater health and overall well-being.

Finding the Love of Your Life. A look at how to be a person someone can live with for a lifetime. Also, keys for discovering that special someone.

Feeling Whole in a World of Couples. Encouragement for singles, and suggestions about how they can find worth and value in their singleness through Christ.

Getting Your House in Order. A practical look at organizing the home and family members' time.

Life with Spice. For years the women's ministry at Community Church of Joy struggled to get off the ground. Finally, we dropped the traditonal denominational program and used a new one called "Life With Spice." It has been a huge success. This once-a-month meeting includes a light dinner, an ice breaker, a special feature like a craft or style show, and a Bible study centered on a topic of interest to women. The invitational, non-threatening, contemporary atmosphere draws women in and encourages them to bring their friends.

Step Together. A seminar on how to build relationships in step-families.

Video Seminars. Many well known leaders and speakers have developed video classes and seminars. These videos provide high quality teaching in a non-threatening environment. The key to success lies in finding the right host or hostess to welcome people and build relationships. Local Christian bookstores should have information on this growing segment of Christian education.

Small Groups. Small groups can serve on many levels, ranging from providing an entry point into the church, to helping people move deeper into faith. Small groups are effective because they offer an intimacy and accountability that larger groups cannot. Opportunities can include activity-based groups (athletic teams, hiking groups, craft groups, volleyball groups, and so on, designed with an intentional time of Bible study or devotions) to growth groups (based on need-oriented Bible studies) to support groups (mentioned above). Many denominational publishing houses and denominational offices offer small group resources.

Entry Level Volunteer Opportunities. Serving as an usher or greeter, or helping on cleanup days encourages participation and growth. The more involved people become in serving, the more ownership they experience in their faith and church. Volunteer opportunities connect people to the church and to others in the church.

Doors to Involvement: Growing Deeper

Most congregations offer in-depth Bible studies. The following titles might stimulate some new ideas or at the very least, new marketing strategies.

Amazing Grace. A study of Galatians.

Get Smart. A look at the wisdom of Proverbs.

Keep the Faith. The book of Daniel.

How to Be A Christian and Still Enjoy Life. Philippians.

Hope for the Imperfect. Romans.

The Plain Truth About Jesus. John.

Worship and Praise in the Psalms.

Understanding the Holy Spirit. A Biblical overview on how the Holy Spirit relates to us today.

Joyful Journey. An in-depth look at the New Testament, its main characters, and basic teachings.

Between the Times. A survey of life and faith in the centuries between the Old and New Testaments.

World Religions. A comparison of Christianity with the major religions of the world.

Exploring the Cults. A comparison of Christianity with the major cults of the world.

C. S. Lewis Book Study. C. S. Lewis wrote several books that make for a stimulating discussion group or class.

Lutheran: To Be or Not to Be. (Substitute the word *Lutheran* with any other denomination.) Today, most people choose churches based on the worship and ministry style rather than on denominational affiliation. As a result, newcomers might be unfamiliar with the teachings and history of the congregation. Yet many, having found a new church home, want to know what the church stands for and believes.

Digging Deeper. This Bible Study, based on the day's sermon, immediately follows the worship service. It enables people, after hearing the message, to dig deeper into the text and theme of the pastor's sermon.

Evolution and Creation. A Bible-based look at two ways of looking at how the world came to be.

Scripture, Prayer, and Singing. Learning how to pray and to sing the Scripture.

How to Discover God's Will. An important topic for all followers of Christ.

Prayer and Fasting. How to enjoy and experience the power of prayer and fasting.

Prayer Journaling. Tips on how to use a prayer journal to enhance one's prayer life.

The Joy of Intercession. Biblical keys for learning how to pray on behalf of others.

A Midweek Believers' Service. A growing number of congregations use Sunday morning worship as a front-door introduction to Christianity geared to seekers. To enable believers the chance to worship in ways that might feel foreign—and intimidating—to the newcomer, these churches provide a mid-week or Sunday night service. The needs of believers set the agenda for this worship experience. The service offers an extended period of time for worship, prayer, and a Bible-study oriented message.

Volunteer Opportunities. Activities that call for greater time commitment (for example, singing in the choir or teaching a class) give people a chance to grow in their faith. A commitment to living out our faith through serving encourages growth.

DOORS TO INVOLVEMENT: EQUIPPING FOR SERVICE

Discover Your Spiritual Gifts. Through Bible study and gift surveys people begin to discover their unique, God-given gifts. They also have the opportunity to put those gifts into action by volunteering in the church.

How to Give Away Your Faith. Insights on how to build loving, caring relationships with people—the starting point for effective witnessing. The course includes tips on how to verbalize one's faith.

Compassion and Care Training. This class teaches the skills necessary to be a lay minister in the area of pastoral care. Skills include listening and praying, along with learning how to us some diagnostic tools.

Other equipping classes and seminars can include training for teachers, communion servers, hosts/hostesses, ushers, prayer team members, small group leaders, visitation teams, and any other area of service in the church. Providing a biblical foundation, an exciting vision, and practical skills makes these classes effective and the time well spent. The better equipped people are for service, the more likely they'll stay committed to the task.

DOORS TO INVOLVEMENT: GOING OUT INTO THE WORLD

Only the imagination of church leaders and members can limit mission opportunities. The following is a small list of possibilities:

Serve food to the homeless; develop a center for those without food and clothes; build a home through Habitat For Humanity; send a group to Mexico under the sponsorship of the denomination or other mission organizations; arrange "Vacations with a Purpose" for people who want to use their time off to serve in a mission opportunity locally, nationally, or internationally; send young people to Russia or other locations to perform dramas and music on the streets; invite friends to worship or other entry-level events; sponsor missionaries; adopt children in other countries by supporting them financially once a month; support denominational missions work by praying for and financing it; invite denominational missionaries to address the congregation; put up a bulletin board about the mission work of the church and denomination that includes opportunities to serve; establish groups that meet regularly to pray for countries around the world; sponsor mission weekends in which the worship services focus on mission opportunities, and so on.

Mission opportunities can also serve as side door evangelism tools. For example, a church member might invite an unchurched neighbor to help install plumbing in a home the church is building for a homeless family. Through the involvement with that mission, the unchurched person finds a sense of fulfillment, meets some great Christian people, and might decide to check out the church.

APPENDIX B

FOR FURTHER READING

•

ANDERSON, Leith, *Dying for Change: An Arresting Look at the New Realities Confronting Churches and Para-Church Ministries* (Minneapolis: Bethany House Publishers, 1990).

ANDERSON, Leith, *A Church for the 21st Century* (Minneapolis: Bethany House Publishers, 1992).

BARNA, George, *The Power of Vision: How You Can Capture and Apply God's Vision for Your Ministry* (Ventura: Regal Books, 1992).

EASUM, William, *Dancing with Dinosaurs: Ministry in a Hostile and Hurting World* (Nashville: Abingdon Press, 1993).

HUNTER, George G. III, *How to Reach Secular People* (Nashville: Abingdon Press, 1992).

KALLESTAD, Walt, *The Everyday, Anytime Guide to Christian Leadership* (Minneapolis: Augsburg Fortress, Publishers, 1994).

KALLESTAD, Walt, and SCHEY, Stephen, *Total Quality Ministry*™ (Minneapolis: Augsburg Fortress, Publishers, 1994).

KALLESTAD, Walt, and WRIGHT, Tim, *Reaching the Unchurched: Creating the Vision, Planning to Grow* (Minneapolis: Augsburg Fortress, Publishers, 1994).

MEAD, Loren, *The Once and Future Church* (Washington, D.C.: The Alban Institute, 1991).

ROOF, Wade Clark, *A Generation of Seekers: The Spiritual Journeys of the Baby Boom Generation* (San Francisco: HarperCollins, 1993).

RUSSELL, Cheryl, *The Master Trend: How the Baby Boom Generation is Remaking America* (New York: Plenum Press, 1993).

STROBEL, Lee, *Inside the Mind of Unchurched Harry and Mary: How to Reach Friends and Family who Avoid God and the Church* (Grand Rapids: Zondervan Publishing House, 1993).

WRIGHT, Tim, *A Community of Joy: How to Create Contemporary Worship* (Nashville: Abingdon Press, 1994).

NOTES

•

AN INVITATION

1. The *Church Membership Initiative (CMI): Narrative Summary Findings* (sponsored by Aid Association for Lutherans, Appleton, Wisconsin, 1993) reports that in 1990 about 250,000 people were "released from membership" in Lutheran congregations. These numbers represent back-door losses and do not include transfers and those who dropped out but were not officially released. The report goes on to say that if trends continue an additional 2,500,000 are likely to join the ranks of Lutheran back-door losses in the next ten years.

CHAPTER 1:

IT'S A NEW DAY AND A NEW WORLD!

1. Cheryl Russell, *The Master Trend: How the Baby Boom Generation Is Remaking America* (New York: Plenum Press, 1993).
2. Ibid. p. 22.
3. Ibid. p. 32.
4. Ibid. p. 56.
5. Ibid. p. 57.
6. Kenneth L. Woodward, "Dead End for the Mainline?", *Newsweek*, August 9, 1993, p. 48.
7. Russell, p. 156.
8. Ibid. p. 50.
9. Wade Clark Roof, *A Generation of Seekers: The Spiritual Journeys of the Baby Boom Generation* (San Francisco: HarperCollins, 1993), p. 67.
10. Ibid.
11. For two excellent discussions of this trend please see *How to Reach Secular People* by George G. Hunter III (Nashville: Abingdon Press, 1992), and

The Once and Future Church: Reinventing the Congregation for a New Mission Frontier by Loren B. Mead (Washington D.C.: The Alban Institute, 1991).

12. Hunter, p. 32.
13. Peter Drucker, *Managing the Nonprofit Organization: Principles and Practices* (New York: HarperCollins, 1990), p. 3.
14. Ibid. p. xiv.
15. While witnessing goes beyond the scope of this book, it is crucial in growing a church. I recommend the following two resources for helping members envision their mission and reach out to their friends:
• Win and Chip Arn, *The Master's Plan For Making Disciples* (Pasadena: Church Growth Press, 1982). The book and/or training kit can be purchased through:

Church Growth 2000
1921 S. Myrtle Avenue
Monrovia, CA 91016
1-800-423-4844

• Paul Sorensen, *Sharing Your Faith with Friends, Neighbors, and Relatives* (Minneapolis: Augsburg Fortress, Publishers, 1995). A small group study.

CHAPTER 2:

Defining Your Mission

1. Ray Bakke, *The Urban Christian: Effective Ministry in Today's Urban World* (Downers Grove: Intervarsity Press, 1987), p. 57.
2. Norman Shawchuck, et. al., *Marketing for Congregations: Choosing to Serve People More Effectively* (Nashville: Abingdon Press, 1992), pp. 57, 58.
3. Ibid. p. 91.
4. Ibid. p. 89.
5. Ibid. p. 91.

CHAPTER 3:

Targeting Your Audience

1. Wade Clark Roof offers a picture of the secular population by looking at the religious preferences of Baby Boomers. He divides them into three categories according to their church involvement or lack of it: Loyalists (33%), Returnees (35%), and Dropouts (42%). He says that two-thirds of all Boomers raised in a religious tradition dropped out during their

teens and early twenties.

Through the years **Loyalists** have remained committed to their religious institutions. During the social upheavals of the 1960s they were the least likely to lose confidence in the country. They were also the least likely to get involved in the counterculture of that decade. They hold to traditional lifestyles and values. They tend to feel somewhat more content with their lives and feel much less need for excitement. Loyalists draw on traditional moral and religious categories. They stress growing **up in** the faith.

Returnees hold more moderate attitudes toward social institutions, exhibiting some skepticism but not as much as dropouts. More alienated than Loyalists from institutions in the 1960s and 1970s, they find congregations strange—filled with odd beliefs, practices, and people who live differently than they do. They tend to be more committed to lifestyle freedom and choice than Loyalists. They speak in psychological or experiential terms and look for feeling-oriented congregations. They stress growing **in** the faith. Returnees represent great potential for mission-driven congregations because of their interest in coming back to the church.

Dropouts, though alienated from institutions, still hold deep, personal beliefs. Their faith feeds on private and family experiences rather than on what religious institutions have to offer. Their personal beliefs do not intrude into the broader social realms. Seventy-four percent of all Dropouts prefer to be alone to meditate rather than worship with others. Roof, *Generation of Seekers*, pp. 154-155, 188-191, 193-198.

2. Hunter, *Secular People*, pp. 41-42.
3. George Barna, *The Barna Report, 1992-1993* (Ventura: Regal Books, 1992), p. 69.
4. Kenneth L. Woodward, et. al., "Talking To God," *Newsweek*, January 6, 1992, p. 39.
5. Jeff Gordinier, "Ona Ka-ching! and a Prayer: In the Wake of 'Gump,' the Entertainment Industry Gets Spiritual and the Profits are Heaven-Sent," *Entertainment Weekly*, October 7, 1994, p. 36.
6. Cheryl Russell, "Predictions for the Baby Boom: Boomers Will Embark On a Spiritual Quest," *The Boomer Report*, July 1994, p. 4.
7. Gordinier, p. 40.
8. Saddleback Valley Community Church, led by Rick Warren, a Southern Baptist pastor, ministers in an upper class, fast-paced California suburb

called Mission Viejo. Baby Boomers populate the area. Through re-searching its community the congregation has developed the following composite of the person it seeks to reach. "Saddleback Sam":
• is a well educated young urban professional
• is self-satisfied and comfortable with life
• likes his job and where he lives
• is affluent and recreation conscious
• prefers the casual and informal over the formal
• is interested in health and fitness
• thinks he is enjoying life more than 5 years ago, but is overextended in time and money and is stressed out
• has some religious background from childhood, but hasn't been to church for 15 or 20 years
• is skeptical of "organized religion"
• doesn't want to be recognized when he comes to church
9. Russell, *The Boomer Report*, July 1994, p. 3.
10. George Barna, *The Frog in the Kettle: What Christians Need to Know About Life in the Year 2000* (Ventura: Regal Books, 1990), p. 137.

CHAPTER 4:

CONNECTING WITH SECULAR PEOPLE

1. Garry Trudeau, "Doonesbury," *The Arizona Republic*, Sunday, March 20, 1994, the comic section. Copyright © 1994 Universal Press Syndicate. Reprinted by permission.
2. Lee Strobel, *Inside the Mind of Unchurched Harry and Mary: How to Reach Friends and Family Who Avoid God and the Church* (Grand Rapids: Zondervan Publishing House, 1993), p. 70.
3. Roof, *Generation of Seekers* (SanFrancisco: HarperCollins, 1993), p. 156.
4. Ibid.
5. Ken Woodward, "A Time to Seek," *Newsweek*, December 17, 1990, pp. 50-56.
6. Russell, *The Master Trend*, pp. 137, 143.
7. Strobel, p. 170.
8. Martin Luther, *Luther's Works, Volume 53* (Philadelphia: Fortress Press, 1965), pp. 62-63.
9. "Common Evangelical Terms Unknown to Most in Survey," *The Arizona Republic*, Saturday, March 12, 1994, p. E5.
10. Gerald J. Hoffman, *How Your Congregation Can Become a More Hospitable Community* (Minneapolis: Augsburg Fortress, Publishers, 1990). This

workbook provides fifteen inventories and other materials to help churches evaluate how outsiders will perceive their ministry.

CHAPTER 5

MORE THAN GETTING THEM IN THE DOOR

1. Peter L. Benson, Carolyn H. Elkin, *Effective Christian Education: A National Study of Protestant Congregations—A Summary Report on Faith, Loyalty, and Congregational Life* (Minneapolis: The Search Institute, 1990), p. 3.
2. Ibid. p. 16.
3. Ibid. p. 17.
4. Ibid. p. 4.
5. Ibid. p. 58.
6. The Charles E. Fuller Institute of Evangelism and Church Growth offers several different spiritual gift surveys. Among the more popular ones are the *Wagner Modified Houts Questionnaire* and the *Trenton Spiritual Gifts Analysis*. The Trenton survey is designed specifically for liturgical churches. For more information contact the Fuller Institute at:
   P.O. Box 91990
   Pasadena, CA 01109-1009
   1-800-999-9578

THE PROFILE OF A DISCIPLE

1. Special thanks to Lyle Schaller for his helpful insights on this survey.

TRANSFORMING A CONGREGATION INTO A MISSION

1. Cynthia Scott and Dennis Jaffe, *Managing Organizational Change* and *Managing Personal Change* (Menlo Park: Crisp Publications, Inc., 1989).

POSTSCRIPT

1. From *House at Pooh Corner* by A. A. Milne, copyright © 1928 E. P. Dutton, © renewal 1956 A. A. Milne. Reprinted by permission of Penguin U.S.A.

APPENDIX A

1. Letter to the Editor, *Virtue Magazine*, November/December, 1993, p. 11.

For information regarding Community Church of Joy's annual evangelism conference or its Resource Center, please call or write:

Community Church of Joy
P.O. Box 6030
Glendale, AZ 85312
(602) 938-1460
(602) 938-9210 (fax)